CAMP GRANNY

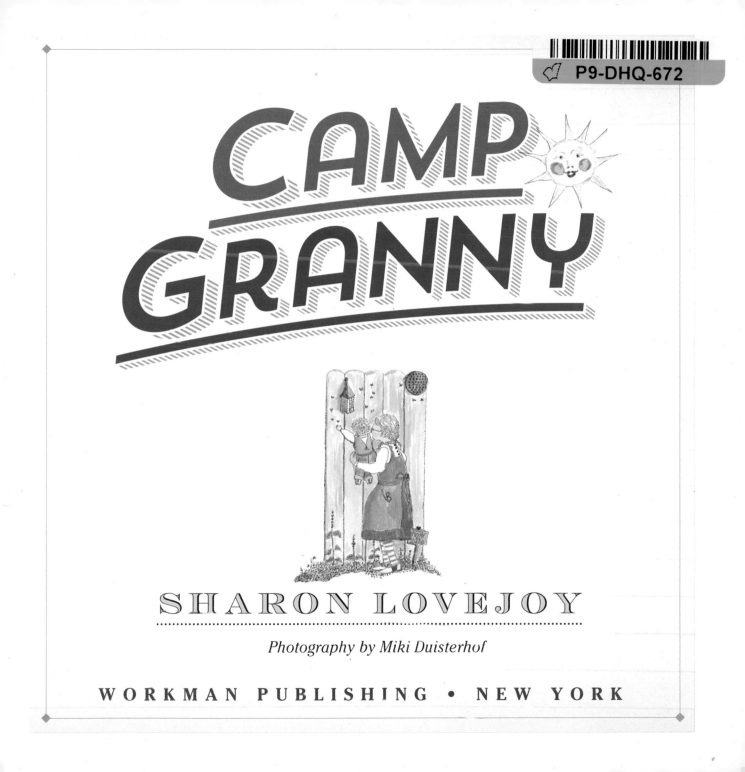

SHARON LOVEJOY

Photography by Miki Duisterhof

WORKMAN PUBLISHING • NEW YORK

Dedication

To my unforgettable Grannies—
Augustine Feller Clarke and Abigail Baker Lovejoy—
All that is good in me sprang from them.

Library of Congress Cataloging-in-Publication Data is available.

ISBN 978-0-7611-8730-1

Originally published as *Toad Cottages & Shooting Stars.*

Workman books are available at special discounts when purchased in bulk for premiums and sales promotions as well as for fund-raising or educational use. Special editions or book excerpts can also be created to specification. For details, contact the Special Sales Director at the address below or send an email to specialmarkets@workman.com.

Workman Publishing Co., Inc.
225 Varick Street
New York, NY 10014-4381
workman.com

WORKMAN is a registered trademark of Workman Publishing Co., Inc.

Printed in Malaysia

First printing December 2009

10 9 8 7 6

ACKNOWLEDGMENTS

How did I get so lucky to be paired with an editor who is not only brilliant and sensitive, but also totally in tune with my way of viewing nature and life? Ruth Sullivan seems to know unerringly what fits, what works, and what is important to the life of a manuscript. We spent dozens of hours on the phone these past two and a half years and every minute was a learning experience. She brings out the best in me and she has molded this book into what you'll read here. Heartfelt thanks.

Peter Workman is one of my heroes. Thank you, Peter, for your belief in my work. Thank you, Maisie Tivnan, art designers Janet Vicario and Amy Trombat, production editors Carol White and Julie Primavera, photo director Anne Kerman, and photographers Miki Duisterhof and Tiffany Howe.

Now to the women who have contributed: Gladys Marie McKinstry, Betsy Williams, Victoria Greene, Bonny Spencer, Mary Rae Means, Sharon Aderman, Aggie Goettie, Kathie Ohmer, Jeanni Montgomery, as well as Cathi Arnold, Sue Eiler, Kim Moreno, Molly Chappellet, Judy Thelen, Cindy Rankin, Susan Branch, Virginia Holihan, Marilyn Brewer, Kary Gonyer, Lynn Karlin, and Jane and Lee Taylor.

My family deserves special thanks for their help. Moses John, Sara, Ilyahna, and Asher, you were great. Jim Prostovich, you were a saving grace. Noah, Lea, and Danielle, you've done a wonderful job. Thanks also to my aunt, Rose Lovejoy.

This book wouldn't exist today if it had not been for the unwavering love, support, and help of my husband, Jeff Prostovich. He gave me the courage and resolve to persevere and to tell my stories. What a life we've shared!

CONTENTS

1 CUP

INTRODUCTION

The bower of jasmine beside my studio is cloaked with snowflake-white blooms. Its scent stops me mid-stride and pierces my heart, as only scent can do, with memories of the two beloved women who changed me forever and for good.

My grandmothers, "Nonie" Clarke and Grandmother Lovejoy, were the first and most profound blessings of my young life. In their loving presence, I felt as though everything I talked about, accomplished, or experienced was important. They may not have approved of or understood some of my actions, but they never overlooked them. Instead, they offered words of encouragement or perhaps guidance to a better pathway. I knew that they always had time for me no matter what was happening in their busy lives.

My first home was nestled into an orchard in my Grandmother Lovejoy's garden just steps from her cottage. Gnarled apricot, guava, fig, and peach trees skirted with jasmine and dianthus leaned toward Grandmother's house with outstretched limbs, as though in an embrace. I spent the first seven years of my life running the hollyhock-flanked trails between Grandmother's home and mine.

How could I have been so lucky? A grandmother only a few steps from me and always ready to explore, read, have faerie tea parties, garden, cook,

"It is as grandmothers that our mothers come into the fullness of their grace."

Christopher Morley

At age two Moses is a fearless nature boy who uses all his senses—especially taste—when exploring.

and talk with me about the mysteries of life. We approached every day together as an adventure, filled with the simple joys and discoveries that are fresh and new to a child and that can also make a grandmother feel fresh and new again.

Some days we worked silently, side by side, absorbing the beauty and sounds that surrounded us. I learned that silence can be as deep and instructive as conversation. Only by being silent could Grandmother teach me to tune in and really hear the high *bzee-bzee* whistling calls of the cedar waxwings that frequented her garden. "All things have a voice," she said, "but most people don't take the time to stop and listen."

My Nonie lived only a few miles from Grandmother's house. Nonie and my grandpa visited us every Friday without fail. Nonie and Grandmother loved each other and delighted in their weekly visits. While Grandpa worked on innumerable odd jobs, we puttered in the gardens, played old-fashioned board games or cards, made secret gifts for family and neighbors, and cooked. When the three of us were together, we laughed and played like girls.

Now I am a grandmother, and it is one of the truest and purest joys of my life. The traditions, stories, cooking, gardening, arts, and patience of Grandmother and Nonie stream through me and eddy around the eager young children who fill my life with light. Whether we are picking berries or storytelling, I feel an invisible current of connection to the grandmothers who

The garden faeries have a kindred spirit in Sara May, who leaves gifts and letters for them in her mailbox.

Asher's analytical mind ponders the how and why of everything, even something as simple as a big bubble.

came before me. Though that connection is invisible, it is as powerful and tangible as the jasmine blossoms that pour their beauty and fragrance into my garden.

My situation is certainly different from that of my grandmothers, who had me and me alone as their only grandchild for many years. I am blessed to have four grandchildren (pictured on these pages), who usually receive my undivided attention and always receive my unconditional love.

Although two of my grandchildren are step-grands, there is never a time when I don't feel as though they are my own. They know me as Gramma Sharon, and they don't measure me against the grandma whose blood flows through their veins. I live about 5 minutes from two of my grands and about 20 minutes from the others. Just close enough, just far enough. Despite chaos and calamities, temper tantrums and tears, our times together are joyful, life-changing, affirming, and a constant challenge.

This grandmother-grandchild relationship is not only about what I can do for my grandchildren, but also what they unintentionally do for me. They've given me the gift of the sweetest love I have ever known. They've given me the gift of "child-sight"—the ability to stop, hunker down, and see things through their fresh, young eyes and minds. When I am with them, I am never unhappy, tired maybe, but always filled with the anticipation of the new things we'll experience.

I feel that a grandparent can be more free-spirited and playful with her grandchildren than a parent is with her child. We bend some of the rules. We laugh with them in situations that might have brought on "the wrath" when we were full-fledged mothers. We remember how scary it felt to spend the night in a strange house and that accidents will happen, but it won't be the end of the world as we know it. We're easier and more resilient, and our hard edges have been rounded and softened by the buffeting of life. As long as my grandchildren need and want me, I just want to be there with an open mind, open arms, and an open heart. What could be better?

I wish for you, my readers, the simple joy and connection that a life with beloved elders and grandchildren will provide. Live fully in each moment, keep journals of precious words and insights, and continue the invisible current for the next generation to pass on to their grandchildren.

Grandmotherhood is a state of grace, a chance to be a child again, to be whimsical, to dance, to sing, to explore, to believe, and to scatter your love, like glistening drops of warm spring rain, onto your grandchildren.

Blessings to you and your
lucky grandchildren,

Sharon Lovejoy

"You must never stop being whimsical."

Mary Oliver

If asked to describe Ilyahna, I would use one word—creative.

"The heart is like the mind, has a memory,
and in it are kept the most precious keepsakes."

HENRY WADSWORTH LONGFELLOW

PREPARING CAMP GRANNY

My grandchildren surge through our kitchen door like a tumbling stream, laughing and calling excitedly, as though visiting Amma's house is the best thing in the world. That's exactly how I want them to feel and how I felt whenever I ran the pathway of hollyhocks to my Grandmother Lovejoy's cottage or threaded up the ribbon of walkway to my Nonie's bungalow. My heart would pound in anticipation. I never knew what we were going to do, but I always knew that I could count on something out-of-the-ordinary to happen—not an extraordinary experience like panning for gold or discovering a new comet, but something wonderful, simple, and memorable that could happen only with a caring and loving grandmother.

WELCOME to CAMP GRANNY

Sara May and I discuss the unfathomable mystery of tooth faeries.

A grandchild's visit is one of the greatest adventures for a grandmother, but it can also be a bit daunting. You may wonder how you're going to fill all the hours between waking and sleep, but luckily the most important ingredient for success is *you*. Lucky you. You're in for an unforgettable experience.

Running a successful and fulfilling Camp Granny isn't about having a giant flat-screen television with 300 channels, a big swimming pool, or the latest computer games—it is about you and the time you share with your grandchild. My friend Nana Bonny hosts her long-distance grandchildren often, and for her, the experience is all about time together and time in nature. On their first morning, she greets her grandchildren with a cup of hot cocoa and a quick trip to the beach to watch the day begin. "We like having our footprints be the first ones in the sand." A grandchild doesn't forget an experience like that.

Your time together is magical, an accretion of memories, stories, traditions, and simple pleasures that, when cemented together through the years, make for one of the most important relationships of a child's life. I guarantee that the strong and loving foundation you build during your visits, or when you're an attentive long-distance grandma, will nurture your grandchild throughout a lifetime.

MAKE WAY FOR GRANDKIDS

Set aside an area that belongs to your grandchild. It can be as small as a drawer, a child-sized table, or a corner of a room (my grands like to hide out under an antique bed), but to your grandchild, it will feel like a home away from home.

A Room (or Drawer) of One's Own

To make her visiting grandchildren feel welcome whenever they spend the night, my friend Gramma Sharon Aderman lays a new T-shirt or pajamas on top of the bed and rests a paper plate "head" on the pillow. The "face" is either an enlarged photograph of the child's face, or a drawing of the child with a fringe of yarn hair. This simple tradition tickles and comforts a child who may not be used to being away from home.

If your grandchild is scared of the first "sleepover," pitch a child-sized tent next to your bed. That way your grandchild is having an adventure, feels protected and secure inside the enclosed tent, and has Granny just an arm's length away. Tuck in a flashlight and include a favorite book or one that you've just discovered. It is exciting to sneak a midnight read by the light of a flashlight.

Dedicate a drawer to each grand so that they always have a change of clothes or pajamas when they come to visit. Such a small thing to do, but it makes a child feel like a true part of your household.

Nana Bonny didn't have enough space in her bedroom for a tent, so instead she turned her closet into a "little room" and outfitted it with a sleeping bag, blankets, pillows, and a flashlight for her grandson, who loved the treat of staying in that cozy space.

This tall bed serves as the perfect indoor hideout and playhouse for my grands, who spend hours hidden beneath it.

Grandma's Bag of Tricks

Whenever you're out on a walk, be on the lookout for great natural things to stockpile for your grandchildren's visits. Since many of the treasures you can use for craft projects are only available during a certain time of the year, collect and store them until your grandchild arrives. Then, on a rainy day (see "Rainy Day Activities," page 167) or a starry night, when you've exhausted all other modes of entertainment, drag out your bag of tricks for craft projects, mini faerie landscapes, or as games, toys, or subjects for drawing and painting.

The Life Board

Hang a big bulletin board, which we call a "life board," on the wall and dedicate a section to each grandchild. Tack the child's initials above his space, add a recent picture, and any art or other projects you want to display. When a youngster away from home sees a space dedicated to him, he immediately feels a sense of belonging. You'll find that your grandchild will make things especially for the board and, upon arrival, will always check it to see what you've featured.

Who Is That Scarecrow in the Garden?

Before your grandchild visits in the summer, prepare a look-alike scarecrow to greet him. Ask his family to save some of the clothes (especially a favorite piece of clothing) your grandchild outgrew and send them to you in advance of his arrival.

Stuff the clothes with straw or crumpled newspaper in plastic bags that are tied closed. Use an old pair of panty hose, some fabric, or a gourd to make the head. Enlarge a current photo of your grandchild, laminate it, and glue it to the head of the scarecrow. Fill the head with stuffing and attach it to the neck of the clothing. Mount the body on a crossed pole in your garden. Place a hat on the scarecrow's head, and scatter some sunflower seeds or peanuts on the brim to attract birds.

Treasure Trove of Games

Build up a treasure trove of simple-to-play children's games like Bingo, Pick-Up Sticks, playing cards, and board games. Keep the games visible in your living room or family room for frequent use whenever your grandchild visits. These games help a child learn sportsmanship, problem solving, interactive play, self-control, communication, motor skills, and more. So turn off your television and video games, and play.

The Book Basket

Fill a basket with books for you and your grandchild to read aloud together. Buy the ones you love and borrow others. You may have kept some of the children's classics that you and your children shared together. If so, reading them to the next generation will bring back fond memories and may lead to new discoveries. The local librarian is well versed in what books are suitable for every age and can help you choose some to check out before a visit. While at the library, pick up *How to Get Your Child to Love Reading* by Esme Raji Codell, which will steer you onto a course of good reading for every area of interest and all ages of children. Esme also gives good advice about reading out loud to children: "Make read-aloud time special. Gather around. Turn off the lights, turn on a cozy lamp . . . flop on pillows, be comfortable, be intimate. Love the book before you read it to children."

Keep a supply of good books in every room—even the bathroom.

The "Mad Basket"

My friend Mary Rae Means showed me a "mad basket" that she and her granddaughters made to help them deal with life's little ups and downs. They sat together and the girls told her what people can do to make themselves happy. Each suggestion was written on a small slip of paper and dropped into the basket. Whenever the girls were mad or sad, they closed their eyes, reached into the basket, and pulled out a scrap of paper with a suggestion, such as, "Hug each other," "Jump around the room on one leg," "Dance," or "Sing your favorite song." They so loved the "mad basket" idea that they made them for other family members and gave them as gifts. Even a curmudgeon would find it tough to be grumpy when a family member is jumping up and down on one leg singing "Eensy Weensy Spider."

Basket of Memories

Keep a big, flat, open basket on your coffee table within reach of little hands. Fill it with photos of your grandchild and other family members. Sit close to the basket and pick up photos, pass them to your grandchild, and talk about the person or animal pictured. Soon your youngster will turn to the basket without prompting from you. Our family photo basket is one of the first places our grandchildren head when they visit. They love to paw through the photos and look at them. Even when my grandson Moses was a year and a half old, he looked closely at the photos and passed them around. This basket will get much more use than a family scrapbook stored on a shelf.

Dress-up Drawers

In the children's room, I keep a small chest of drawers that I stock with wonderful clothes, hats, crowns, old costume jewelry, worn-out watches, shirts, old glasses, evening purses, sunglasses, and the biggest hit of all, a long reversible cape, dark on one side, shiny red satin on the other. Both the boys, who become magicians and sorcerers, or the girls, who are princesses, queens, or faeries, use the cape whenever they can.

I scout out long pieces of fabric— from velvet to satin, inexpensive swaths of nylon netting, and cotton—that can be wrapped and tied to make skirts, shawls, and cloaks. My grandchildren dress up in their costumes when they're playing make-believe or performing for a family gathering. It is amazing to see the transformation that occurs, not only in their voices, but also in the way they assume different characters and accents.

CROWNS AND WIZARD CAPS

Using the patterns and instructions on page 200, make a heavy paper cone and a crown. They're great for dress-up and a birthday crown makes the day very special. Cut out stars and a moon from light paper and glue them in place. Spread a thin layer of glue on them, and sprinkle with glitter dust.

Visit thrift shops, dance stores, and flea markets for a range of quick costumes.

Your Journal

When my granddaughter Sara was a toddler, I invested in a lovely, handmade journal for writing my memories about her. I inscribed these words by Mary Oliver on the back page of the journal:

"What is it you plan to do /
With your wild and precious life?"
Every time we were together and she said a new word or did anything out of the ordinary, I wrote about it in the journal. As grandmothers, we always think we'll remember the time we first heard a special word or saw our grands do something memorable, but our memory banks are already fairly full, so it's good to write those things down.

On each of my granddaughters' birthdays, I glue a colorful envelope onto the page of the day and tuck a piece of family jewelry, a photograph, or special memento inside. I seal each envelope so that when they're opened, many years from now, they will be a complete surprise for my grown-up grandchild.

Set aside some quiet moments alone to record your memorable times together.

Fabric of Your Grandchild's Past

By the time my first grandchild was born, most of my beloved aunts and uncles, grandparents, great-gran, and others had already passed away. I felt this broad hole in the fabric of our history and somehow wanted to introduce my granddaughter to multiple generations of her family.

For a month, I spent evenings sifting through boxes of ephemeral treasures and amassed a few dozen old photographs, some from as far back as the late 1800s. One rainy day, I sat in my studio and carefully put together a photo album, which included names and a bit about each person.

Nothing touches a child's heart like storytelling, so I wrote a short story or family history to go along with each of the photos. For example, to accompany a photo of her great-great-grandpa John Clark riding his favorite horse, I wrote, "Here is your great-great-grandpa who was the last of the Arizona Rangers. He rode this horse through the Arizona Territory at the beginning of the twentieth century and searched the Grand Canyon for bandits." I am amazed by how my grandchild remembers the stories, takes them into her life and history, and retells them to others. Through this, I feel that our family still lives and will as long as their stories are remembered and passed on.

A Birth Tree

Plant a birth tree for your grandchild somewhere in your yard or in a large pot. Introduce the child to his birth tree, take a photo of the two of them together, and measure their heights. Let your grandchild water and feed the tree whenever he visits. Start a photo journal of the two of them, and keep track of their growth through the years. You'll be surprised by how important the tree will become to your child.

This sunflower—planted for me by a bird or squirrel—appeared in a bucket of soil.

The Sunflower Snack Bar

If you are going to plant just one pot of flowers in anticipation of a grandchild's visit, make it big, broad-faced sunflowers. You can put the seeds into the soil as early as April, and the plants should be up and blooming within two months.

Small varieties and giant sunflowers can be planted in a large container filled with bagged potting soil. Sunflowers' broad faces will attract butterflies, skippers, and bumblebees all day long. And, at night, they will lure amazing moths (see page 68) to the nectar on their disk blooms. Sunflower leaves make delicious salads for hungry birds. In the fall, the dried sunflower heads can be set out to feed the birds.

Memories in a Time Capsule

Start amassing artifacts for a family time capsule that you will bury together. Find a sturdy box with a tight-fitting lid and tuck in some old toys, a coin with the current date, a letter from your grandchild with a current photo, a family photo with the date noted, a picture of a family pet and a story about the pet, some important newspaper headlines, or a news magazine front cover and story. Make a recording of your voices and sing a song together. Voices change constantly, and the memorable yet ephemeral sound of a loved one's voice is to be treasured.

Find an area outdoors that isn't destined for a construction project or any other disturbance. Seal your box of artifacts in an airtight container like a lidded plastic box or Rubbermaid container, and bury it at least a foot deep. Stick a pole or stake into the ground above the capsule to mark its whereabouts (believe me, you think you'll remember where you buried it, but you won't). Wait a couple of years (or longer) before unearthing your time capsule. You'll be surprised by how exciting this is for a youngster, and by the changes that have occurred.

Tokonoma for Two

Many years ago, a friend told me of the Japanese tradition of keeping a *tokonoma,* an alcove in her home for the display of scrolls, flowers, natural objects, and pieces of art. The arrangement is usually changed daily, which helps keep senses fresh, aware, and stimulated. When our surroundings remain static, we stop seeing things, even when they are beautiful and rare.

I began the custom in my own home, taking time out from chores to find an opening flower, the castanet seedpod of a jacaranda tree, a scattering of sea-washed mermaid's tears (sea glass), or whatever was wonderful and new to my eye. Now, when my grandchild comes to visit, it is a special treat for her to seek out natural objects for the *tokonoma* display in the hallway. Each new arrangement or single item is perfectly placed, admired, and appreciated fully.

When you are outdoors with your grandchild, you might point out something that would be nice for the *tokonoma,* but leave it to him to decide what items he wants in the display. Your job is to step back and admire and praise.

The fleeting beauty of a branch of apple blossoms will take center stage in your tokonoma.

Mud Pies & Sand Castles

Most grandchildren aren't with their grandparents enough time to warrant a sandbox, which might be used only once or twice a year. But sandboxes and kids go together like peanut butter and jelly, so here is a short-term solution. Purchase play sand from a garden center or home- and landscape-supply store. Fill a large wheelbarrow or a small child's swimming pool with the sand, a bucket, dishpan, cups, shovels, a plastic squirt bottle full of water, spoons, pots, and plastic bowls.

Nothing beats a fresh, handy mud puddle for making the best mud pies and to add variety and texture to sandbox projects. Fill a big bucket or container with gooey mud, and set it close to

Anytime is tea-party time when a Granny and grandchild are together.

the sandbox. You'll be amazed by the hours your grandchild will spend outdoors making mud pies, building sand castles, even mini mud cities.

Note: In case neighborhood cats visit your sandbox, cover the sand with aluminum foil, newspaper, or a piece of chicken wire. Cats can't stand to walk on the foil, paper, or wire, and it thwarts their attempts to dig.

A Child's Own Tea Set

When I was a child, my grandmother often celebrated our lazy summer afternoons together with a cup of tea (mine was mostly cream) and some cookies or a freshly baked bit of pie crust sprinkled with cinnamon sugar. Grandmother had a grown-up teapot, cup, and saucer, and I had a miniature Chinese-style blue willow tea set, which fit perfectly into a small picnic basket.

I so cherished our beloved tradition of sharing teatime together that when my granddaughters were born, a miniature tea set in a basket became one of my first purchases. By the time the girls were two and a half, they were old hands at the art and ceremony of tea parties, and they even spoke with amazing British accents. So, although I don't normally urge anyone to spend money, I do hope you'll find the perfect tea set for your grandchild, and then invest in the time to have a tea party and a treat whenever you two have the chance to play together.

FAERIE ADVENTURES

Faerie Mailboxes

Whenever I ran into Grandmother's garden as a child, I'd head straight for the sycamore tree. Would I find another little gift from the garden faeries? One day when I knelt beside the hole at the base of the tree, I found a small box filled with brightly colored stones. When I rushed indoors to show them to Grandmother, she dropped the rocks, one by one, into a water-filled gallon jar on the breakfast-nook table. During the day, we watched as the rocks miraculously changed from little lumps into a forest of rainbowed stalagmites. How did those faeries always know what would tickle the imagination of a young and curious child?

The wonder and joy I felt whenever I discovered those hidden treasures stayed firmly planted in my memory. I wanted to start my own tradition of faerie gifts for my grandchildren, but didn't know exactly what to do. One day in a craft store, I stumbled across some miniature galvanized tin mailboxes that looked just like the real thing. They even sported little flags, which the faeries could raise whenever they left a gift inside. We painted each box a different color—purple for Ilyahna, pink for Sara May, bright yellow for Asher, and red for Moses. You could also make a mailbox out of wood and custom paint it with your grandchild's name and favorite color.

Painted wishbones, decorated leaves, shells, flowers, and other natural objects are favorite gifts from the faeries.

We mounted the mailboxes on fence and porch posts in hidden areas throughout the yard. As soon as the children arrive for a visit, they sprint through the garden straight to their mailboxes to check for surprises from the faeries.

I try to make the faeries' gifts small, homemade, and as natural as possible, though sometimes I tuck in magical stickers, wooden toys, mini magnifying glasses, or dollhouse accessories. Once I made a purse out of a skeletonized tomatillo husk that I beaded and decorated with golden thread. Another time I put together a miniature tea set out of love-in-a-mist pods and acorn caps. I often write leaf notes from the faeries using Pilot silver and gold pens (fine point) to make them seem magical. No wishbone is ever wasted here; they're painted, tied with silver and gold threads and bells, and left inside the mailbox for my grandchildren's wishes.

What is really wonderful is that now my grandchildren often leave thank-you notes and gifts for the faeries. They're learning how important it is to give as well as to receive.

BUILT-IN FAERIE MAILBOXES

You already have a built-in faerie mailbox if you have a tree with a hole in it. If possible, make a tiny door to cover the hole, and construct a mini flag to hang from a twig to indicate when the faeries have been there.

A painted wishbone is cradled in a velvety pelargonium leaf and sprinkled with faerie dust.

Faerie Play

As a child, I spent countless hours building faerie houses, making miniature faerie gardens, and serving pretend tea and food to my wee unseen visitors. My neighborhood friends, both boys and girls, slipped into the moment and gathered snails for slow-paced faerie chariots, picked an array of blooms for clothing and crowns, and helped serve tiny foods made from mud and colorful flower blossoms.

I've found this child's faerie play to be universal, from the dappled woods of Sweden to the hidden forests of Monhegan Island, Maine, where children and grown-ups create magical faerie houses using only nature's toy chest for materials. When given a chance to play outdoors, children inevitably invite the faeries to be a part of their lives.

I watched in awe as my granddaughter Ilyahna laid out a perfect faerie landscape under the pine tree. Her stockpile of leaves, flower petals, twigs, moss, acorns, shells, and pods were fashioned into beds, rugs, tiny chairs, and dishes fit for even the most discriminating of faeries.

The strange thing is that she did this before I had the chance to teach her about making a faerie garden. I had been looking forward to initiating her into the ways of the faerie-folk, but like most children, she was privy to all that knowledge without needing any help from a grown-up. She instinctively reached for some of the beautiful and natural objects scattered throughout the yard and began the quiet and joyful work of creating magic.

Children lose themselves in the miniature world of faeries and their homes and gardens.

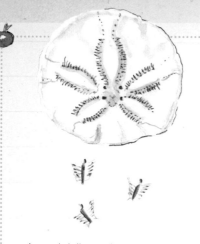

A sand dollar makes a great tabletop. When a sand dollar is broken, little white angels fall out.

Faerie House and Garden

You can make faeries a part of your grandchild's life by providing some areas for play and a ready supply of natural objects. Before your grandchild arrives for a visit, set the scene for a faerie landscape. Find a shaded area of your yard (under big bushes or trees) and clear a circular space for your grandchild's hidden faerie garden. Smooth the soil and outline the circle with pinecones, acorns, twigs, shells, or rocks. Plant the circle with a collection of small bulbs or coral bells, a plant the faeries love. Fill in the circle with a cushion of soft mosses or mulch.

Be on the lookout for wonderful shells, pebbles, rocks, pods, cones, twigs, lichen, mosses, and leaves—anything that would work for outfitting a faerie house and garden. Around the time of a child's visit, nestle your natural finds throughout the yard or garden and near the cleared faerie space.

When your grandchild arrives, walk outside together and discover the magical circle. Stroll through the yard and find some of the natural objects you've seeded there. As you gather them, talk about what they look like and what they might become in a faerie garden or house.

Leaf flag

FOR CITY GRANNIES

Don't despair if you live in an apartment or somewhere that doesn't have a garden. You can create a mini faerie garden. One of my best faerie gardens was made in a 2-by-3-foot wooden box (left) filled with soil, topped with moss and lichen, and outfitted with woodland and seashore finds.

Faerie Home Furnishings

Wherever you look outdoors, you'll find natural treasures to build and furnish a faerie house.

Chinese-lantern floor lamp

Pussy willows for faerie pillows

Curled leaf chaise with woolly lamb's ear for an afghan

Hollyhock footstool

Chestnut bed and rose petal blanket

Scallop-shell headboard

Leaf-and-twig tepee

Rosehip teapot and acorn cups

Acorn birdhouse

Pinecone scales for shingles

Teapot with grapevine handle and spout

Mussel-shell bathtub

Thin rounds of branches for tables

Berries for architectural embellishments

Sycamore "button" for a modern lamp

Love-in-a-mist sugar bowl

LONG-DISTANCE GRANNY

Not all grandmothers are lucky enough to have their grandchildren living nearby. Time together may be limited to holidays or a long summer visit, but a faraway grandmother can still play an important part in the life of her grandchild. The simplest remembrances, conversations, letters, and traditions can keep the intimate bond between a grandmother and child flourishing across the miles.

Put a Face on the Long-Distance Granny

Gramma Sharon Aderman showed me the way she refreshes her youngest (and too far away) grandchildren's memory of her. She had photos of the faces of herself and Grampa Jim enlarged, mounted on cardboard, and pasted to paint sticks, which she sent to her daughter. Whenever she calls her grandkids, her daughter and son-in-law hold the photos up so that the grandchildren associate the voices with the pictures.

Send a photo of you and your grandchild doing something together to your grandchild's parents and ask them to use it as a screen saver. Some screen savers constantly scroll through a series of photos. You'll find that your grandchild will see the photo and talk about the experience with his parents. And your memory will remain fresh in his mind.

Use a favorite photo as a screen saver.

A Grandchild's Personal Book-of-the-Month Club

Make a habit of sending your grandchild a book a month. Focus on special subjects that you may encounter when you're together. For example, these inspirational faerie stories would make a good choice before you begin building faerie houses and gardens: *A Fairy Went A-Marketing* by Rose Fyleman (recently reprinted), the Fairy Houses series by Tracy Kane, and *Fairy Island* by Laura and Cameron Martin.

Over the Hills and Through the Woods

I always want to hear from my grandchildren, but when they sit in front of a large sheet of stationery, they feel daunted by the prospect of having to fill the entire page. To navigate around this fear, I go to the local art and craft store and buy small pads of watercolor-weight blank postcards. They're the perfect size, and they are great for your grandchild's paintings or drawings. If you can't find these pre-made postcards, cut out your own from watercolor paper. Address the postcards to yourself, stamp them, and give them to your grandchild. Ask his parents to encourage him to sit down and write or draw you something every couple of weeks. Have someone photograph you holding the card when you receive it, then tuck the photo into your next letter to your grandchild. Though you are out of sight, a steady stream of letters and photos means you'll never be out of your grandchild's heart. Keep the handmade cards in a personal scrapbook. The next time you're together, you can read the cards aloud.

Handmade postcards will track the life, interests, and skills of your young artist through the years.

If a birthday falls on a date when you're not together, you can create an event anytime.

Making Birthdays Special

A CARD FOR EVERY YEAR

Years ago, Grammy Marilyn Brewer showed me a stack of birthday cards she was mailing to her granddaughter Kara. "On every birthday, I send a card for each year in Kara's life." What grandchild could ever forget a grammy who flooded the mailbox with cards? They can be homemade, so the only expense is paper, envelopes, stamps, and time.

CELEBRATE AN UNBIRTHDAY

My granddaughter Sara May's birthday comes in midsummer when I am living in Maine. She was always so sad to have me miss her special day, but I remedied the problem by making it a tradition to celebrate her birthday a month in advance. I do it just as I do for the other grandchildren: decorations, a birthday banner, a fancy cake (in her favorite color), party favors, and of course gifts. She no longer mourns my absence. Two birthdays a year is exciting for any child.

The next time your grandchild asks if you'll be attending the big birthday celebration, assure him that although you won't be there at the party, you will have another birthday extravaganza the next time you're together.

REMEMBER OTHERS

Buy or make a family address book for your grandchild and include cousins, aunts, uncles, in-laws, and good family friends. Fill out all the information from A to Z, including each person's birthday. When you are with your grandchild, take out the book and look for birthdays to remember. Start this tradition even before your grandchild begins school. Make simple cards with drawings or let your grandchild call or send an e-mail. This is a great way to teach your grandchild to give of time and love whenever possible.

An Old-Fashioned Letter

Whenever I am away from home, I send my grandchildren a weekly letter—a real letter, sealed in an envelope and written with love and care. I want them to know that they are always in my heart and mind. I tuck small gifts inside each envelope, and many times I illustrate the notes with small sketches or paintings, and use silver or gold markers instead of pens.

Hi Asher—
The [porcupine] decided to feast on our big birch tree last night! We can't wait for you to see one up close, but not too close!

I miss you!
Love,
GS

Sara May says my garden is "magical," but you Moses—think of it as one big grocery store filled with your favorite fruits.

Since your first steps you have wandered our garden—grazing your way through every area.

You love the loquats so much that you'll even munch on the ones almost gone by. Yikes! I watch you closely & even at this early age show you what is safe & what is poisonous.

Sara May learns quickly, as I am sure you will.

I Love you Moses,
Your Amma

...couldn't help thinking of ... "Chicken Girl" when I ... into the poultry barn ... Common Ground Country Fair ... all the varieties.

You would've loved the mama ... with her two chicks ... led on her back. I've seen ... own chicks do the same thing!

I miss you! Send me a letter soon!
Love xxoo— GS

Family photos keep memories alive for generations. Be sure to date the back of every photo and identify each person.

Ties That Bind

How do you keep those memories of your times together alive when your grandchild lives far away? Whenever you're together, take photographs of your adventures, meals, journeys, and projects. (Do it so often that your child becomes oblivious to the camera-wielding grandma.)

After your grandchild leaves, use your talents to make a vacation book of your adventures. Write a story about your good times, put in some of your grandchild's direct quotes, and add a liberal dose of photographs throughout. Send the completed book to your grandchild for a holiday or birthday.

Old Memories

Grandchildren love to see old photographs of their parents when they were their age. Every holiday, find a family photograph that corresponds with the age of your grandchild, enlarge it, paste it onto a card, and mail it to your grandchild. The old photo is guaranteed to stir up memories and stories.

Photo Ops

Send an inexpensive plastic camera to your grandchild and include a pre-addressed and stamped padded envelope for its easy return. Equipped with a camera, a child feels important and powerful and will gladly snap photos to share with Granny. So when you ask your grandchild to show you what her life is like by taking pictures of her friends, pet, school, and trips, you will surely get a response. Have her parents mail the camera back to you, so that you can get the film developed and share in a part of her long-distance life away from you. When she visits, you can talk about the pictures.

A Good-Night Story

Whenever you and your grandchild read together, take note of the most beloved stories—the ones you're asked to read over and over. After your grand leaves for home, record some of the short stories to send to him. As you read, ask direct questions, such as, "And, what did the tiger say?" or "How did the people react when the spider dropped down in front of them?" The questions allow your grandchild to participate in the story just as when you read in person. Send your recorded good-night stories in an "I already miss you so much" box, which may also include a small recorder (digital or tape) and some simple mementos of your time together.

Spend a quiet morning recording your grandchild's favorite stories.

For some reason, fortune cookies and grandchildren are a perfect match. My grandkids love to break into the cookies at the end of a meal and share their fortunes with us. Keep a supply of the cookies in your cupboard and use them as an impromptu dessert *and* a bit of entertainment.

Your life will be happy and peaceful.

Keep in Touch

BOOKMARK-A-MONTH

Once a month, make a special bookmark for your grandchild and send it to him. Choose a family photograph, a photo of a favorite pet or place to visit or a favorite book or food—anything that will remind your grandchild of your good times together. Laminate the bookmark so that it will last.

WORD-A-MONTH STUMPER

Ask your grandchild to send you a favorite word of the month. Encourage her parent to help the child peruse the dictionary for funny and unusual words or ones that are difficult to use in a sentence. The object is to stump Granny, who must write back a funny sentence using the grandchild's word. Some of my favorites so far have been stupendous, flabbergasted, dilly-dally, and nincompoop (see the book *Carmine: A Little More Red* by Melissa Sweet for some great words).

JOKE-A-MONTH

Collect a selection of jokes specifically targeted to your grandchild's age. Once a month, call your grandchild and tell her a joke or email her parents with a joke from you. Chances are your grandchild will have a joke to fire back at you.

COMMEMORATE THE DAY

On the day your grandchild is born, purchase a copy of a magazine or newspaper with the date. When he is older, you can pull out the

We read 13 books on the afternoon you visited me— Hurrah! xx OO Amma

Remember all your great adventures in the tide pools? You were afraid of the crashing waves, but your Daddy protected you— xx x OO Amma

Our good neighbor Marti Morse snapped this as we paddled out of Little Harbor. We watched as the fox trotted across the bridge to Birch Island. xxoo Amma

paper and let him read about what happened on the momentous day he was born.

On the Way to Granny's House

My grandchildren are fascinated by the road atlas we keep in the backseat of our car. They love to pull it out of the seat pocket and follow the route from our house in California to our cottage on an island in Maine. They get excited by the names on the map, the cities, the rivers, and the ocean, and they ask questions about areas of the United States that they've never visited. The questions inevitably lead us to many tales about our journey to Maine and the places to visit along the way. Maps are a great way to give your grandchild a knowledge of and easy familiarity with the faraway place that he will (hopefully) visit someday.

Select a map of the country to send to your grandchild, and use a marker pen to highlight the way to your house. Indicate places you visited along the way from his house to yours, and include photographs of special places you might visit together someday (zoos, botanic gardens, museums, rivers). As you travel, send a postcard from each place you stop, telling stories of the adventures you're having en route.

GRANNY'S TRAVEL BAG

I dreaded the car travel that was usually a big part of family vacation time. Grandmother Lovejoy solved the problem of my boredom by fixing up a special travel bag, which I couldn't open until we had been on the road for at least a half hour. Once an hour, after the initial opening, I was allowed to reach inside the closed bag and fish out one thing. Usually it was something simple like a set of magnets, a peel-back Magic Slate, tiny coloring books and crayons, Old Maid or Go Fish playing cards, or a notepad for playing hangman or tic-tac-toe. No matter what she supplied, I was always thrilled and the little travel bag of tricks kept me contented for hours.

TRAVELS WITH GRANNY

Elderhostel and many museums and organizations now offer special grandparent-grandchild tours for families. Grandtravel.com, established in 1986, is devoted to educational tours exclusively for grandparents and their grandchildren. Their intergenerational trips are not only fun, but also teacher-led, imaginative, and richly educational.

TECHIE GRANNY

Stay in touch with your tech-savvy grandkids. Facebook, Twitter, Skype, FaceTime, Instagram, text messages, and emails keep you just a keystroke or click away from your grands.

Bubbles at the Ready!

If there's one thing you always want to have on hand for whenever your grandkids arrive, it's bubbles. No true grammy would ever be caught bubble-less. Even older kids love to play with them, and they're easy to make from the common household ingredients below. Bubbles store well if kept tightly lidded in the cupboard.

GRAMMY BREWER'S HOMEMADE BUBBLES

2 cups water (distilled water works best)

½ cup blue Dawn (not Ultra) dishwashing detergent

¼ cup light corn syrup or glycerine (found in skin care sections of pharmacies)

Gently stir the ingredients together and try not to create foam. Pour the mixture into a lidded plastic container and store it overnight before using. Mix gently and pour the bubble mixture into a tub or large plant saucer. Dip a wand in and blow!

JUMBO BUBBLES

6 cups distilled water

2 cups original Blue Dawn (don't use Ultra)

1 cup light corn syrup

For a big party, you'll want to make a super-duper batch. Use a small, clean tub (Rubbermaid makes lidded 3-gallon tubs, which are about 11 inches by 16 inches). Pour the ingredients slowly into the tub and mix gently and thoroughly trying not to create foam. Use a giant, homemade bubble wand to stretch and trail your jumbo bubbles.

Keep your bubble supplies in an accessible area within easy reach of little hands.

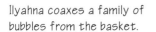
Ilyahna coaxes a family of bubbles from the basket.

Asher tries for a prize-winning sausage-shaped bubble.

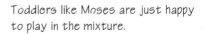
With wet fingers, Sara can blow big bubbles without a wand.

HOMEMADE BUBBLE WANDS

Stretch a coat hanger into an elongated circle. Wrap the handle in tape to prevent scratches on little hands. Wrap the circle of the wand in cotton string or chenille stems, which will absorb and hold more solution for longer blowing. Use plastic strawberry or tomato baskets to blow clusters and strands of conjoined bubbles.

BUBBLE MAGIC

Dip your hands into the soapy water and you'll be able to gently poke your finger into the side of a bubble without popping it. Fill a jar lid with your bubble solution. Dip a drinking straw at an angle into the bubble mixture until it is wet halfway up the straw. Now carefully (without letting your lips touch the bubble solution) insert the wet straw into a bubble and blow gently. You'll blow a big bubble and if you wet your finger and poke it into the bubble you'll form a family of little bubbles.

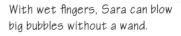
Toddlers like Moses are just happy to play in the mixture.

"One of the luckiest things that can happen to you in life is, I think, to have a happy childhood."

AGATHA CHRISTIE

CHAPTER TWO

The NEIGHBORHOOD NATURALIST

My Grandmother Lovejoy taught me that nature isn't something only enjoyed on a vacation or a drive to far away, but that it is everywhere around you. You'll find it in the most obvious and unlikely places—in the corner of the living room where the spider spins, in your backyard where the worms wriggle silently through the soil, or in the night skies where fireflies flicker and meteor showers scribe the blackness with streaks of glittering light.

When you share nature with your grandchild, there are no rules that say you must know the answer to every question or the name of every bird, plant, or insect you discover. Sometimes the shared curiosity and then the journey of looking for answers are more exciting than the answers themselves. Experiencing nature together means that you open yourselves, like blooming flowers, to the myriad mysteries unfolding around you.

BACKYARD EXPLORER KIT

- A big (unbreakable) magnifying glass

- Drawing pad or journal

- Colored pencils or crayons

- Inexpensive camera

- Binoculars (a 7 x 35 or 8 x 50 lens is fine for viewing, but a 12 x 60 would be better)

- Headlamp (for nighttime viewing; some are equipped with a red bulb)

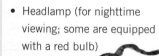

- Small tape or digital recorder

Keep these items in a bucket or basket close to the back door so they are always handy.

Set aside time to walk with your grandchild very slowly around your yard or neighborhood and tote along your Backyard Explorer Kit for close inspections. Remember to cultivate patience and approach your shared adventures with a child's anticipation. Stop whenever and wherever your youngster shows an interest in something. Hunker down close to the object, look at it together with a magnifying glass, and talk about it. Don't rush from point to point with your thoughts on the finish line. Slip your grown-up perception of time into the filaments of your grandchild's life until the two are woven together as finely as an oriole's nest.

A magnifying glass is one of the best ways to tune a child into the tiniest things in nature.

A FIVE-SENSES WALKABOUT

When you're sharing nature with a child, you'll find that even a short walk through your backyard will yield a crop of fresh discoveries and questions. Start a tradition of asking, "I wonder what's going on outdoors today?" then grab your grandchild's hand and your Backyard Explorer Kit and step outside. Look under rocks or push aside leaves, and you're likely to find some roly-poly bugs, a beetle, or maybe a worm or two. Use your magnifying glass to look closely at a handful of soil or the insect-busy face of a sunflower or cosmos blossom. Move from sunny to shady spots to find a variety of flowers, trees, bushes, and critters. You'll cultivate a new awareness and appreciation of even the tiniest happenings, and you'll give a gift of curiosity that lasts a lifetime.

When my grandchildren were babies, I would carry them from plant to plant, tree to bush, letting them touch, see, smell, taste (only things I *knew* to be safe), and listen to the goings-on in the backyard. We didn't need to know the proper names of things; we just enjoyed experiencing them. Our walks became a tradition, just as the walks I shared with my grandmother became one of my most cherished memories. No matter your grandchild's age, now is the time for you to become a child-at-heart and reexamine the world from his or her perspective.

Birdbaths are a powerful magnet for birds of all kinds.

STOP AND LISTEN

Close your eyes and *listen*! Try to identify and describe as many sounds as possible. Do you hear the wind through the needles and leaves of trees? Some trees have such distinct "voices" that when their leaves are windblown, we can recognize the kind of tree we're hearing. Stand near a pine and listen to the whispering of the needles. Listen to the wind rushing through cottonwood, poplar, or aspen leaves, which sound like crackling fires, or oaks, which sound like rustling taffeta skirts. Can you hear birdsong, hummingbird wings, bumblebees rumbling, grasshoppers snapping as they leap, dragonflies clattering together in battle, water dripping, children yelling, music playing, or cars honking? Ask your child, "What do you hear? Can you hear the . . . ? Can you make that kind of sound?" Imitate the varying sounds and try to count how many there are.

SNIFF

Forget about your dignity and lead your youngster on a snuffle, snort, and sniff walk around your yard, neighborhood, or a park. You'll sound like a dog on a trail, but you'll find scents everywhere that you may have overlooked—even rocks sometimes have a scent. Crush mint leaves in your hand. Sniff the newly mown grass, the blooming roses, or the perfume of blossoming fruit trees. How does a plant smell when a leaf is crumpled or when a twig is snapped? Do ripening strawberries or apples have a fragrance?

TASTE

Visit areas of your yard, neighborhood, or a U-Pick farm, where there are edible herbs, fruits, or vegetables, and take time to *taste* and savor. Describe which of the five tastes you're experiencing. Is it sweet, sour, bitter, salty, or *umami* (Japanese for "delicious")? The *umami* taste is noticeable in the core flesh and seeds of a yummy, ripe tomato.

At this moment in time, there is only the strawberry.

LOOK

Talk about the myriad colors and shapes you can see outdoors. Describe the specific colors: not just green, but chartreuse, lime, sage, silvery, or olive—the nuances are endless. Use colored pencils or crayons to duplicate the objects and the colors in your nature journal or drawing pad. Don't worry about how the drawings look; just play with the colors and shapes. Look for natural patterns in rocks, leaves, shells, and even windrows of sand. Pick samples of differently shaped petals and leaves and bring them home to study or to paste into your nature journal.

TOUCH

Run little hands over velvety leaves like lamb's ears, rubbery succulents, tasseled grasses, suede moss, stubbly lawn, lichens, tree bark, flowers, and herbs. Dip your fingers in the water of last night's rain puddle. Talk about and sample the tickling, prickling, soft, ridged, pliable, stiff, crumpled, woody, smooth, flexible, warty, bristly, granular, wet, and clumpy things surrounding you. Jot some quick notes in your nature journal about what you saw and how things felt when you touched them.

If this kind of close observation is new to you, too, you've given yourself (as well as your grandchild) a gift—you'll never go outdoors again without seeing and feeling things in a fresh way.

Children naturally want to touch everything they encounter.

Sensory Sack

One of my favorite ways to help children really "see" things is to take them on a gathering expedition with a sensory sack. Give each child a large brown paper sack or other container. Take a leisurely walk and have each child gather a dozen objects, such as cones, seeds, leaves, shells—any natural thing with an interesting shape, texture, or scent. As they pick up articles, they should drop them immediately into their sacks, keeping them tightly closed and opening them only when adding to them. No fair peeking—just drop the finds inside and keep going.

When you return home, each collector (one at a time) sets his closed sensory sack on a table and moves around the table to a new place in front of a sack filled by another child. Tie a bandanna around the first child's eyes, open the sack slightly, and let him reach inside and grab one article. After he takes time to feel it, he describes it to the other players, and guesses what it might be. (Write down the answer and silently give ten points for each correct guess.) Finally, let him lift it out and onto the table. Repeat the process until the sack is emptied; then take off his bandanna and let him see the objects. Give the child his score. Let each child have a turn with one of the sacks. This simple game is not only fun, it helps children develop their communication and observational skills, and even practice a bit of math.

Children become totally immersed in nature when they are on a mission.

Tabletop Nature Museum

My grandmother encouraged me to collect natural treasures for a "nature table" she designated on the dining room buffet. Even the most common and overlooked bits of nature proved fascinating—things like the nectar pathways inside flowers, the tiny barbules on owl feathers, and the pearly operculum (trapdoor) of a moon snail we found on Catalina Island. We researched the identity of things we didn't know and made a label for each piece with the name, date, and location where we found it.

Whenever you go outside together, take along a bucket or basket to gather your own treasures. Dedicate a table to display the wonderful things you've collected. Research the identity of all you find and any unusual qualities, stories, or natural history attached to them. Keep a box of field guides and 3-by-5-inch cards nearby to help make identification tags for your "museum" treasures. You might want to pick a theme of the week—for example, heart-shaped rocks, acorns, pinecones, and seeds. You can build your own bird's nests as we did by collecting twigs, grass, moss, and lichens, and mostening the fibers to mold them into nest shapes.

Change your "museum" displays weekly and take time to discover exciting facts about the objects.

Nature Map

Spend an afternoon with your youngster drawing a map of your yard or neighborhood on a large sheet of paper. Draw a tiny house where your home is located and indicate any special features of the landscape such as a tree house, pond, dead tree, outbuilding, or fence. Post the map on a bulletin board, wall, or in your child's hideout (see page 46).

Whenever you walk together, take along your notebook and keep track of where you discovered something notable, such as a turtle sunbathing, a spider spinning an orb web, crows mobbing a hawk, or a patch of blooming flowers—anything that attracts your child's attention. When you return home, pinpoint on the map where you made new discoveries. Help your child draw the critters, flowers, or trees on the map where you saw them, add comments to the map, and date your discoveries.

After a few seasons of adding to and keeping your nature map, you'll find that the natural cycles (nesting, migrations, blooming of flowers, fruiting) repeat during the same time period each year. Keeping a nature map fosters a child's intimacy with her surroundings and opens her eyes to the untold mysteries and happenings in even the smallest yard or most crowded neighborhood.

Start your map in your own backyard so your grandchild will feel familiar with her surroundings.

Leaves, Leaves Everywhere

Next time you are out on one of your expeditions with your grandchild, make a point to notice the variety of leaf shapes in bushes, trees, and vines. Some maple and fig leaves resemble hands; cottonwood and redbud leaves are perfect hearts; magnolia leaves are tough and leathery enough to paint on. Sassafras have leaves like mittens, and elephant's ear plants have leaves like . . . you guessed it! Look down at the tiny ground-hugging violets with sweet, heart-shaped collars. Examine the rhubarb's parasol, the nasturtium and lady's mantle capes, and the fennel's ferny foliage. Every leaf has its own signature shape and texture, and sometimes, as in the case of fennel, its own scent.

Take a leaf walk on a dry day and collect a basket of the best specimens. Look for different shapes, sizes, and colors. When you get home, brush the soil off the leaves and spread them on a table with the vein side up. Look at them through your magnifying glass. Explain to your child that each leaf is like a little food factory that sips sunlight and gases and turns them into a sugary supper for the plant. The veins are tiny straw highways that transport the sugary supper from the leaves to the plant. Without these healthy veins doing their jobs, a plant would not survive.

When you are out on your leaf-collecting walk, gather leaves for the other art projects described in "Rainy Day Activities" (page 167)—creating a leaf collage, making a natural stained glass window, or making leaf cards for a Mother Nature's Memory Game.

Try doing your leaf rubbings on a sheet of vellum or tracing paper. Tape it onto a window for a magical effect.

LEAF RUBBINGS

Lay a piece of paper over the top of the flat leaves and show your child how to rub the side of a peeled crayon, a pastel stick, chalk, or a soft pencil back and forth across it (be careful not to tear the paper) until you have what looks like a skeleton-view of the leaf.

You can use your homemade leaf paper for a unique and personal gift wrap, stationery, or gift cards. If you do a colorfast rubbing (such as with crayons), you can cut out each individual leaf shape for bookmarks or place cards for a special family meal.

HOME, WILD HOME

Another way you can connect your grandchild to nature is by working together to turn your yard into a friendly gathering place for critters. All you need to provide are three ingredients: food, water, and shelter—which can be as simple as a pile of twigs or as fancy as a painted toad house.

A pond, birdbaths, a diversity of plants, and a layer of straw mulch help make this garden a haven for critters and kids.

Attract Butterflies

Butterflies recognize certain combinations of colors, shapes, sizes, fragrances, arrangement of blooms, and visible and invisible nectar guides to find their food preferences. To attract them to your porch or yard, just plant a pot or plot of some of their favorites such as butterfly weed, cosmos, lavender, or zinnias.

Would you believe me if I told you that butterflies are not only attracted to sweet flowers, but also to fresh piles of dung, rotting fruit, and mud puddles? Why not make a big mud pie to attract backyard butterflies? Butterflies don't drink from open water, so your moist mud pie is the perfect place for them to stop for refreshment.

A butterfly will land and uncoil its springlike proboscis to suck minerals, dissolved salts, protein, and calcium—invisible ingredients they need for successful mating.

MUD PIE RECIPE

Fill a large saucer with soil and sand. Sprinkle on a bit of table salt.

Have your grandchild thoroughly wet the soil to make a mud pie, and then wet it every day—a task she will love. Place a flat rock in the center of the pie so butterflies can land and feed. Drizzle a bit of maple syrup on part of the rock for an extra snack.

Set the mud pie in a sunny area of your garden, preferably near flowers. You might want to spy on your mud pie from inside your hideout (see page 46). If you keep a close watch, you may see all kinds of butterflies, from butter-colored sulphurs, flittery skippers, blues, which look like tiny patches of sky, and yellow-and-black tiger-striped swallowtails—all gathering for a mud pie party.

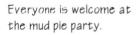
Everyone is welcome at the mud pie party.

Butterfly Mud Pie

HOW TO MAKE YOUR BACKYARD CRITTER-FRIENDLY

To attract an array of beneficial critters to your backyard, make some of these simple animal- and insect-friendly projects with your grandchild.

Set out a basket of feathers, grass, and fibers and watch your birds gather them for their nests.

Orchard mason bees are our native pollinators and not aggressive. Mount a tin can and fill it with paper straws (right) or provide a wood block (below) drilled with $^3/_{16}$-inch holes about $^3/_4$ inch apart.

Phoebes are great bug eaters and prefer to nest on protected porches or special shelves.

Provide a variety of feeders for different birds. This covered tray feeder keeps seed and nuts dry.

Birdhouses encourage future generations.

Drill a $^5/_8$-inch hole in a clay pot for bee entry. Lay dry grass at bottom and cover the top with a flat rock to keep the inside dry.

Mound a permanent stack of rocks for a lizard hotel. Lizards will feast on insects and larvae.

Save some of your flower clippings, bundle them, and attach them to a post to feed a host of birds.

Birds Welcome

Plant a pot of flowers to lure bees, butterflies, flower flies, and ladybird beetles.

Nectar Pot

Plant fennel, parsley, or dill to encourage swallowtail butterflies to deposit eggs. Their young will feed on the host plants.

Box turtles feast on slugs and grubs.

A pond is always the center of activity in a garden. But a half barrel will suffice.

A terra-cotta pot slightly raised (about 2 inches) on a rock will give a toad a safe abode.

Even a saucer of water will encourage insect-eating frogs to visit your gardens.

Sunflowers will attract butterflies, birds, and moths galore for both day and night viewing.

TOAD COLLEGE

Oh, you handsome toad, thank you for eating 2,000 insects a season. Provide him with a pesticide-free garden and a layer of mulch.

Make Room for Hummers

Of all the birds in the garden, I think my grandchildren love the hummingbirds the most. The fearless little hummers think nothing of flying close to children as if to monitor what they're doing. You're most likely to entice hummingbirds into your yard if you and your grandchild plant a big pot or window box of easy-to-grow orange and red tubular flowers like salvia, fuchsia, penstemon, or nasturtium.

A hummingbird feeder is one of the best investments you can make for your grandchild's up-close nature experiences. Hang a feeder in a shady spot in an area you can view from indoors, or attach a suction-cup nectar feeder to your window for some amazing views. Sometimes a feeder will attract numerous hummers that will all vie for a place to sip.

Make your own homemade nectar—it's easy and much better for the birds than the commercial mix with coloring. Combine one part pure cane sugar (never honey or sugar substitutes) with four parts water (never any food coloring). Bring water to a boil or microwave on high for one and a half minutes or until the sugar is dissolved, then set aside to cool. (Store leftover nectar in the refrigerator.)

If you're not having luck attracting hummers, tie a bright red bow to the top of the feeder. Your feeder should be cleaned with a bottle brush and pipe cleaners every four days, then rinsed and rinsed again before filling. Please don't believe the old tale that hummingbird feeders should be removed in early fall. You just may be a lifesaver for a bird who has been blown off course or caught in a storm during its long migration.

Helping to Build a Nest

I remember early spring mornings when Grandmother would tell me to sit quietly as she'd tug a hairbrush through my tangled red curls. At the end of the ordeal, she patiently ran a comb through the brush, lifted out the hair, and tucked it into a strawberry basket, along with short pieces of string, bird feathers, wool, dried grasses, pine needles, and twigs, and placed the basket outside near our breakfast-nook window. Then, we'd sit inside and watch as swallows selected the white feathers for their boxes, jays took a bit of everything for their untidy nests, and goldfinches, towhees, and others rummaged through the contents like shoppers at a flea market.

In the springtime, when birds are getting ready to build their nests, go outdoors together and gather twigs, short pieces of natural fiber, feathers, hair, fur, milkweed down, and grasses. When you return home, spread the fibers on a table and tuck them into a mesh bag (the kind often filled with fruit, potatoes, or onions) or a fruit or suet basket. Hang the container in an area out of reach of cats and out of the elements so the contents stay dry. If possible, hang the fibers near a window or hideout, so your child can see how the birds select and tug out the contents. Then, quietly track the birds with your binoculars. With good luck, you'll be able to see where they build their nests and to watch them incubate their eggs and raise their young.

Our offerings of twigs, twine, leaves, and moss were put to good use in this nest.

Create a Hideout

One of the best days of my young life happened when Grandmother Lovejoy's old refrigerator conked out and she replaced it with a new one. After the movers delivered the refrigerator, we were left with a huge cardboard box that Grandmother said would be my hideout.

My hideout house turned into a perfect spot for spying. I loved peering through the small holes to watch the mockingbird shove food down her noisy babies' mouths. Sometimes, a hummingbird zoomed up to my window and inspected me through one of the peepholes. I spent hours tucked away inside there, immersed in the world of nature but unnoticed by the critters I spied on.

Kids love their own hideouts, a place where they can dream, read, visit with pals, or sometimes just watch what is happening around them. A good hideout, which birdwatchers and photographers call a "blind," is the best way to see nature without nature seeing you.

BUILD A HIDEOUT

Visit an appliance store and ask if you can have one of their large, empty boxes (big enough for your grandchild to stand inside).

1. Stand the box on end and open the four flaps on top. Draw a triangle on two opposing flaps, as shown.

Every child loves a hideout. Moses claims ownership of this appliance-box fort.

2. Cut along the dotted lines with a razor knife and fold the cut flaps up.

3. Fold the uncut flaps up to close the box and form a peaked roof. Use duct tape to seal the top ridge and sides of the roof.

4. Draw windows and a door on the cardboard, score along the sides leaving a side uncut for the hinge. Next, note where your grandchild's eyes are when standing or sitting on the ground and score small openings or peepholes on the sides of the hideout. Use a razor knife to cut through the cardboard, and poke through the scored holes with a screwdriver to open them. You may want to staple nylon screening over the door (leave a flap big enough to crawl through) and the openings to prevent mosquitoes from entering.

5. Have a painting party and coat the outside of your hideout with exterior house paint and decorate it with murals of flowers, bugs, and animals.

Place the hideout in a shady spot near an area used by birds (and other critters) for feeding, drinking, or bathing. Equip it with things like a blanket, water, notepad, binoculars, a magnifying glass for seeing things up close, and maybe even a tape recorder for birdcalls or observations. You might also want to hang a "neighborhood bird chart" (see sidebar, above) to help your grandchild recognize visitors.

NEIGHBORHOOD BIRD CHART

Collect magazines with photographs of birds commonly found in your neighborhood. Help your child cut out the photographs and paste them onto a heavy sheet of paper. Write a little bit about the size and colors of each bird and its habits. Tape the chart near a window or peephole in your grandchild's hideout. He will soon learn to recognize these backyard friends.

Whenever you're bird-watching with your grandchild, look for some telltale identification markers on the birds, such as bright coloration, white patches, bill size and shape, eye positioning, feet, patterns of spots, stripes, or eye stripes. Here is a great way to tell whether you're looking at a hunter—or the hunted:

Eyes to the front,
Born to hunt.
Eyes to the side,
Born to hide.

Hawks and owls look ahead in search of prey. Quail, grouse, and others that are hunted have eyes on the sides of their head to have a wider field of vision.

One way you can get to know birdcalls is by attaching a transparent acrylic feeder to one of your most frequented window areas—close to a kitchen table or reading chair. The windowpane feeders cling to glass with suction cups and are easy to relocate, if necessary. Some bird feeders are especially adapted to thistle seed, sunflower seed, or suet. You'll attract a wide variety of birds by using more than one type of feed. Keep a bird book nearby to help with identification and call recognition.

Whenever you're outside, make a game of listening for bird words and name-callers. Do your best to imitate them. Just call back quickly and you and your grandchild will usually get an immediate reply. Loudly make a kissing noise or a *pish-pish-pish* sound. When you do this, curious birds will often fly near to identify you.

Step outside, close your eyes, and listen to the myriad songs and calls of your neighborhood birds. Some whistle, hoot, say their own names, mimic other birds and animals, laugh, shriek, or sing lilting melodies, and some even say words you may recognize.

Cedar waxwings will visit your yard if it has a supply of berry-producing plants.

Bird Words

jay! jay! jay!

Tune in and try to locate the bird you hear saying these bird words.

"What cheer, cheer, cheer! Chip, chip, birdy, birdy!"

Cardinal

"Drink your tea, ee, ee, ee!"

Eastern towhee

"Who cooks for you? Who cooks for you all?"

Barred owl

"Fire! Fire! Where, where, here, here, see it, see it!"

Indigo bunting

"Old Sam Peabody, Peabody, Peabody!"

White-throated sparrow

"Spring of the year! See you, soon. I will see you. Spring is here!"

Eastern meadowlark

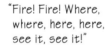

"Teakettle, tea-kettle, teakettle!"

Carolina wren

"Look up! See me: Over here, this way. Do you hear me? Higher still, chewy!"

Red-eyed vireo

"Trees, trees, murmuring trees, 1, 2, 3, I'm lazy!"

Black-throated green warbler

"Chick-a-dee-dee-dee. Feed me, feeeed me!"

Chickadee

"Very, very pleased to meet cha!"

Chestnut-sided warbler

"Three-eight, three-eight, three-eight!"

Yellow-throated vireo

"Beans, beans, beans!"

Common nighthawk

"Teacher, teacher, teacher, teacher!"

Ovenbird

"Witch-ity, Witch-ity, witch ity, witch!"

Common yellowthroat

feed me, feed me, feeeeeed meee

For the Birds: Pinecone Feeders

A variety of feeders and seeds will attract an amazing array of birds.

Collect a few open pinecones to fill with your homemade peanut butter energy food. Hang them in the spring and fall when the weather is cooler. Birds will welcome the high-energy food source.

ENERGY BOOSTER

1 cup crunchy peanut butter
1 cup canola oil
4 cups yellow cornmeal
1 cup white flour
A few teaspoons of shelled sunflower seeds or raisins

Pinecones
Hooks or wire

Your grandchild will be a great help measuring and mixing the ingredients together. Using a knife or spoon, slather it onto and into the open scales of a pinecone. Store leftover Energy Booster in a covered container in the refrigerator.

Screw a hook into each cone at the bottom or tie wire to the top of the pinecones. Suspend the pinecones from branches, porch eaves, or deck railings out of the sunlight.

Scavenger Hunt

I still remember how my heart thumped whenever we set out on one of our scavenger hunts. Although I knew it was only a game, somehow it seemed like the most fun task in the world to find everything on the list and do it faster than the other team.

The game needs at least four players for two teams, but more participants make it even more fun.

Make a list of at least ten nature objects that are commonly found in your area and available that season. For instance, you wouldn't list acorns in June or lilac blossoms in August. Provide each team with the list of items and one large paper bag. Blow a whistle or ring a bell to signal the start, and explain that you will do the same thing when the hunt is over. Limit the scavenger hunt to half an hour. When the stop whistle blows, both teams gather and show what they have. Appropriate prizes are awarded to the winners.

An old-fashioned scavenger hunt quickly turns kids into nature detectives.

LIST OF NATURE ITEMS

1. pinecone
2. heart-shaped leaf
3. roly-poly bug
4. egg-shaped rock
5. feather
6. 3 daisies
7. seeds from flowers
8. 2 fruits or berries
9. fern fronds
10. dandelion flower or puffball

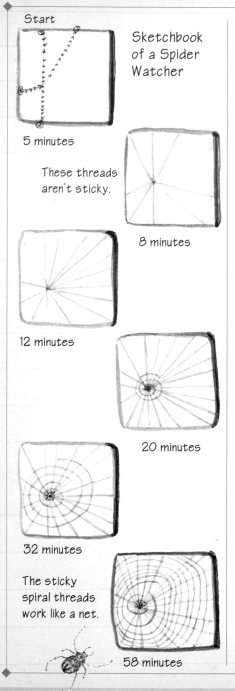

Start

Sketchbook of a Spider Watcher

5 minutes

These threads aren't sticky.

8 minutes

12 minutes

20 minutes

32 minutes

The sticky spiral threads work like a net.

58 minutes

Faerie Handkerchiefs

Early one morning, Grandmother Lovejoy took me outside to her shady front porch. From our perch above the broad St. Augustine lawn, we could see hundreds of gossamer veils blanketing the grass. Grandmother called them "faerie handkerchiefs" and explained that these dew-spangled creations were the sheet webs of spiders. I was terrified of spiders, as are many children. Learning that spiders were the magical weavers of "faerie handkerchiefs" helped me overcome my fears.

Knowledge and familiarity are two ways you can quell some of your grandchild's fears about spiders. You're likely to find spiders throughout your yard, which will make it easy to watch them while they hunt or spin their miraculous webs.

Whenever you explore your garden with your magnifying glass, you'll be able to peek into the quiet lives of a variety of spiders. Look closely along the edges of plant borders, under flower blossoms (where you usually find crab spiders), around trees, in bushes and vines, and on fences. Nearly everywhere you look, there is probably a web and a shy spider hiding out and looking at you.

Different species of spiders have their own style of making webs, from funnels to sheets, hammocks, triangles, thick silk trapdoors (with hinges) atop burrows, tangles, indoor cobwebs, domes, bowls, labyrinths, parasols, sacks, and, my favorite, cartwheel orbs that resemble perfect lace doilies. See how many you can find.

On our Maine porch, our resident orb-weaving spider Seraphina spins her beautiful daily web (left). Seraphina is an *Araneus* and she is related to Charlotte. Sometimes when she twangs at the spiral, she looks like a harp player.

Spider Search

This game, a treasure hunt for spiders, needs two or more participants. Take a walk and carry along a magnifying glass and a pad of paper for scorekeeping. (Score 10 points for each thing you find on this list.)

CAN YOU FIND:

🌀 A spider that looks and walks like a crab?

🌀 A web that looks like a lace doily?

🌀 A spiderweb shaped like a funnel or a triangle?

🌀 A spider dangling from a single dragline?

🌀 A spider "ballooning" through the air on a silken thread as Charlotte's babies did in *Charlotte's Web*?

🌀 A spider carrying her babies, eggs, or an egg sack on her abdomen?

🌀 A spider hiding under a rock or some leaves?

🌀 A silken bundle or "mummy" in a web? Watch a web for a few minutes after a fly or bug is caught, and you'll see how the "mummy" is made.

🌀 A very long-legged spider often found under logs, in the corners of porches, or in sheds and basements? If he gyrates wildly to confuse his prey, he's a vibrating spider.

🌀 A long-legged critter with one fused body part, no antennae, and two eyes? It isn't a spider, but a harvestman. He'll rise up on six legs and wave two legs above his body when he is disturbed.

An *Argiope* awaits her supper.

The spider, dropping from a twig,
Unwinds a thread of her devising:
A thin premeditated rig
To use in rising.

—E. B. White

WATER WORLD

Water is a magnet for children and wildlife. Whether it is a mud puddle for splashing or a pond filled with tadpoles and fish, find a water source and you'll find myriad miracles all around you. My grandkids are happiest when they're rescuing tadpoles from shrinking puddles, exploring tide pools at the ocean, or playing in the creek. Whenever a rock is turned over, new and exciting creatures are uncovered. When a pond is skimmed with a net, wonderful things happen: tiny fish flee, frogs hop to a safe hiding place, water-strider spiders skate rapidly away, and voracious dragonfly naiads, with their huge hinged jaws, strike fear in young hearts.

A dragonfly naiad is a fierce insect that catches fish and tadpoles.

A mayfly lives one day as a fly.

A water-strider spider feeds on small critters.

When you set out on your own waterside expedition, take along a bucket, a dipping net (available in pet, sporting goods, and toy stores), an underwater viewer (directions for making it on page 57), magnifying glass, and a camera. For the best visibility, find a safe, well-lit place for your water explorations, and make sure that your shadow is behind or beside you, but not in the area you're trying to scope out. *Note:* Remember never to leave a child alone near water, not even for a minute.

Slow down, assume a comfortable position, stop moving, and shhhhhh; the more quiet you are, the easier it is to eavesdrop on the critters. You may think that your grandchild doesn't know how to be still, but if you whisper that you need to be as quiet as a spider, your child usually will slip into the mood of the moment.

As the pond dwellers become used to you, they'll resume their lives and you'll be able to watch damselflies catching bugs, swallows swooping in for insects, dragonflies sitting like sentinels atop rushes, and butterflies cruising from flower to flower. The activities are ever changing and endlessly fascinating.

Under the surface of the water, you'll find another world of life. Use your homemade underwater viewer to scope out the activities. For the first few minutes, you may not see anything, but

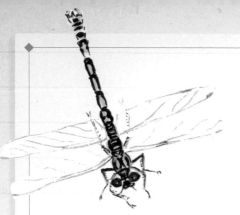

as your eyes become accustomed to this watery habitat, all sorts of things will loom into view. When you spot something exciting, dip it out with a net or jar and examine it with your magnifying glass. You might even take a photo of any odd specimens so you can consult your field guides when you return home. (Remember to return your discoveries to their watery home.)

A gomphid dragonfly perches like a hawk, then flies forth to seize prey and return to perch.

A child will explore a pond or creek for hours.

A stonefly nymph lives in moving water.

A diving beetle is found in ponds, streams, and lakes. Its back legs are like paddles.

A whirligig beetle twirls and wildly feeds on small insects that fall into water.

A water boatman uses its middle and hind legs as oars and front legs to collect algae and plants.

Underwater Viewer

A jar of polliwogs to watch for a few hours.

Whenever you're out together near a pond, tide pool, creek, or lake, use your homemade viewer to get a water critter's view of life.

YOU'LL NEED:

Large #10 can (3 quarts)
1-gallon plastic freezer bag
Thick rubber band

Remove both ends of the tin can. Place the tin can in the plastic bag. Secure the bag with a big rubber band. Slowly lay the can on the water, with the open end up, and watch!

For night spying underwater, find a big jar with an airtight lid. Place a small, lit flashlight facedown inside the jar and screw on the lid. Hold the jar in the water with the beam facing down.

Frogs are great bug catchers.

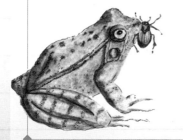

A simple underwater viewer opens up a new world.

My favorite meals were the ones Grandmother tucked into one of her old bandannas and tied to the end of a sycamore stick. I loved hiking around the garden with the stick propped on my shoulder, the bandanna bundle swinging from side to side. Grandmother called this a "bindlestick lunch" (*bindle* is the German word for "bundle"), and every bite was blissful.

Bindlesticks are also an easy way for a young naturalist to carry supplies.

Keeping Track of Visitors

My granddaughter Sara May is the one who taught me how exciting the discovery of animal tracks can be for a child. One day as we were hiking along the creek that flows through our town, she looked down at the muddy bank and excitedly announced that she could see the tracks of a dog. We kept looking and found what looked like bird tracks—delicate hieroglyphics all over a sandy spot near a pool. We were hooked and couldn't stop scouring the ground for clues of what animals had visited.

Since most people don't have a pond or creek in their yard, I devised a simple water feature for the backyard that would not only be a magnet for wildlife, but also would record the tracks of the critters attracted to the water both day and night.

YOU'LL NEED:
Large saucer, tray, or garbage can lid
Sand
Water

Deer

Bury the container up to its rim in soil in a sheltered, shady part of your yard. Surround it with a circle of sand about 2 inches deep and a foot wider than the container. Late in the afternoon, let your grandchild fill the container with water and smooth the sand. Go out first thing in the morning to look for the telltale tracks of animals that may have visited the "pond" during the night. Pat sand smooth again and check often for pawprints. Note in your journal which animals have visited, and encourage your child to make a quick sketch of the tracks it left.

Frog

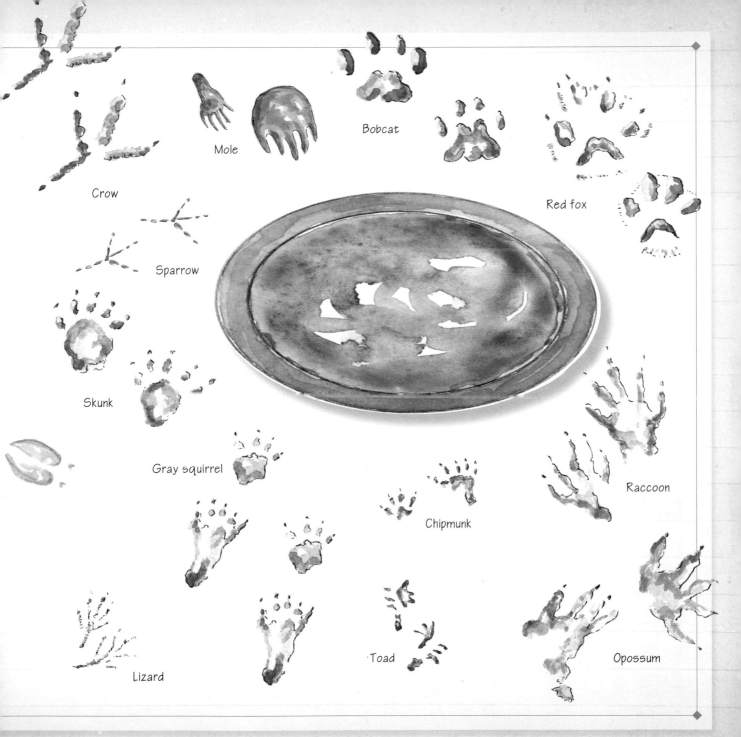

Crow

Mole

Bobcat

Red fox

Sparrow

Skunk

Gray squirrel

Chipmunk

Raccoon

Lizard

Toad

Opossum

NIGHTTIME EXPLORATIONS

When the warm summer night cloaks your yard in darkness, it is time for some exciting, mysterious, and sometimes even scary, night-spying adventures. After the sun sets, bats begin their hunt, clicking above you in a strange high-pitched voice that you can sometimes hear. Moths flutter and dip into flowers, toads ramble bandy-legged through the yard, frogs croak, crickets trill, and owls hoo-hoo-hoot. Darkness sharpens our senses, and maybe it's my imagination, but it seems to heighten expectations, as though adventures are just around that tree, behind that rock, or beside the rippling pond.

LET THERE BE DARK

Have you ever noticed how after only a few minutes of walking in the darkness, our eyes adapt and things around us pop into view? Our human eyes are equipped with cells called rods and cones. The rods are light sensitive, which helps us see in darkness, and the cones allow us to see color. Humans still don't have the great night vision of owls, who have many hundreds of thousands more rods in their big eyes than we do.

Night eyes of a barred owl

So many children are afraid of the dark, yet darkness often yields the best crop of wonder. You and your grandchild should pick up a flashlight and a magnifying glass, and move slowly through your yard or neighborhood. (Choose one special area of your yard for young children or explore the surrounding neighborhood with older kids.)

Moonlight & Eyeshine

Take a little hand in yours, and head out into the night. Shhhhhhh, walk slowly, talk softly, and look, look, look—under leaves, at the tops of grasses, in trees, bushes, and flowers. For best viewing, wear a headlamp (like a miner's light, which is held on the head by an adjustable elastic band) because the light will be at eye level and you'll see the eyeshine that signals the location of hidden critters. **Turn the page to discover what you are likely to see in the dark.**

Moth

Green lacewing

June bug

Skunk

Opossum

Fox

Ferret

Whip-poor-will

Toad

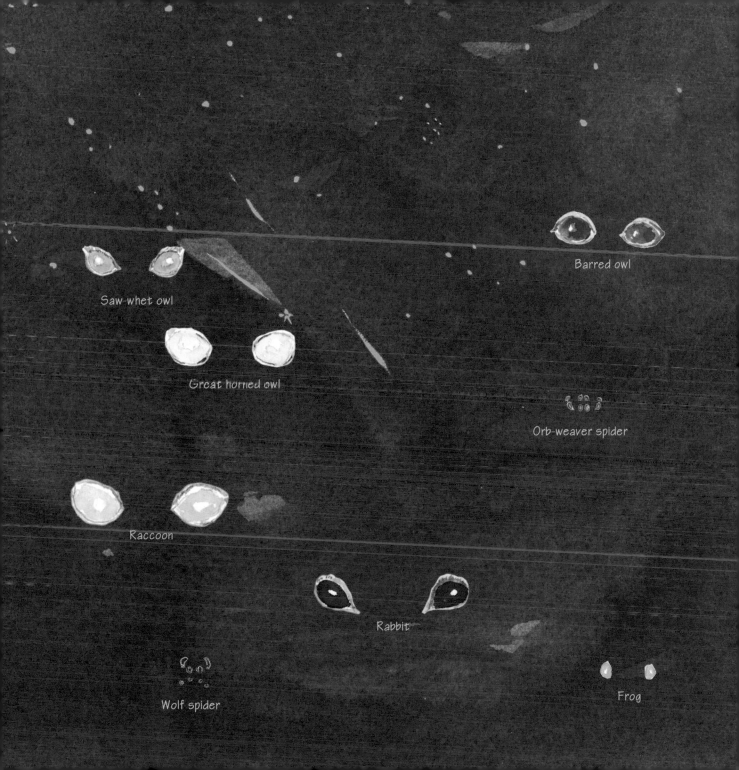

Firefly Lanterns

On a June evening when you see little pinpricks of light flashing in the backyard, go outside to search for fireflies. Look for the flying male's flash and the perched female's answering dash of light. Count how many times in a row the male flashes, and use your flashlight to send identical signals. Watch the fireflies flash in return. They think you're a big firefly in their territory!

In some cultures, fireflies are tucked into carved and pierced gourds to be used as natural lanterns. You can make your own lantern in a screen-covered canning jar. Female fireflies are the easiest to catch because they sit still on twigs and grasses. Capture a few of them gently in a jar, top the jar with a piece of nylon screen secured with a rubber band, and you've got a perfect lantern. Sit in a dark place with your lantern to observe the fireflies. Each species has its own sequence, intensity, and rhythm of flashing. Don't forget to release them before the night is over.

Male (above, right) and female fireflies

The Little Harpist

Follow that cricket's chirp! Cup your hands behind your ears and listen—you're extending your ear power by making them bigger, like rabbits, deer, and foxes. You'll be better able to locate and track a trilling male cricket (only the male sings) to his hideout. Move slowly as you approach, or he'll use his strong jumping legs for a quick escape. Focus your flashlight on him and watch until the trilling resumes. Crickets make their melodic tunes by stridulating—moving a sharp-edged scraper on the outer edge of one wing against the filelike teeth of the other. This action causes a vibration that resonates on a small portion of the wing called the "harp."

If you would like to invite a singing cricket into your home, you'll need a jar, a small piece of nylon screen, and a thick rubber band. Sneak up on one of your backyard crickets, place the jar over him, and slide the screen under him (they usually move for the screen, but grudgingly). Lift the jar and hold the screen in place with the thick rubber band. Use your magnifying glass to look at the cricket as closely as he is probably looking at you. Doesn't he look as though he is wearing an ancient suit of ill-fitting armor?

If you want to keep your cricket indoors for a few days, you'll need to provide a larger enclosure like an aquarium topped by a sheet of screen. Add a layer of soil to the bottom, put in a handful of grasses, some twiggy little branches, and a moist piece of sponge for drinking. Your grandchild will love to feed him with a few bread crumbs and bits of apple or potato—but not too much! Remove the sponge daily, run hot water over it to clean it, moisten it with cool water, and place it back in the cage. You'll be repaid with the insistent chirp-and-trill song of your little visitor. Remember to release the cricket after a few days of watching him.

AN OLD-FASHIONED BURGLAR ALARM

Cricket chirping is so predictable that in some Japanese homes, crickets were kept as burglar alarms. The minute the normally vociferous crickets felt the vibrations of footsteps, they ceased chirping, which alerted their keepers that unwanted guests were in the house.

When I found a cricket in this bean tepee, I encircled it with screen so we could be serenaded for a few nights.

Moon Walks

Moon walks aren't just for astronauts. Go outdoors together for a few minutes every night and look for the rising moon, which comes up in the east and sets in the west just like the sun. It's best to do this at or near the full moon, when the sun sets and the moon rises at nearly the same time. As the full moon wanes (gets smaller), the moonrise will happen about 30 to 70 minutes later each night.

Use binoculars to help your youngster decide if the moon is a laughing man, a happy woman, or maybe even an animal. Use a camera tripod for support, or prop the binoculars on a railing or wall to make for jitter-free viewing. Through the lens, you'll be able to see the mountains, seas, and oceans, which we now know are vast lava plains, highlands, craters (the sites of meteorite impact), and dark lava flow areas. On a crescent moon (a sliver in the shape of a C), look at the dark side to see the ethereal earthshine, which is the sun's reflection off the earth and onto the moon's night side.

Check on the moon during the night. Sometimes, when there are tiny ice crystals in the atmosphere, you can see a glowing halo around it. On other nights, when the full or nearly full moon is rising or setting and there is a fine mist or spray, you might see a

waxing →

1   2   3   4

rare and magical moonbow, which can be pearly white or the faint colors of the rainbow. When the moon is waxing, it is growing and on its way to becoming a full moon. When the moon is waning, it is getting smaller and smaller till it is invisible to us, but it's still up there. Here's how you can easily remember the phases of the moon with hand movements:

Moon points toward the east (cup your right hand into a backward letter C), shine be increased

Moon points toward the west (cup your left hand into a letter C), wane, be at rest.

MAKE A MOON PHASE FLIP BOOK

You'll need at least ten 5-by-8-inch dark-colored cards and a silver marker pen. In the center of each card, draw one phase of the moon until you've done all eight phases that can be seen in a one-month cycle. Label each phase from one, which is the new, or black, moon, to number 8. Color in the moon forms with the silver marker. Make an extra copy of phases 1 and 2.

Staple the ten cards together along their left border, keeping them in numerical order and adding the extra phase 1 and phase 2 to the end. Give the pages a quick flip and watch closely. You'll see a lightning-swift version of the moon phases and the beginning of a new cycle.

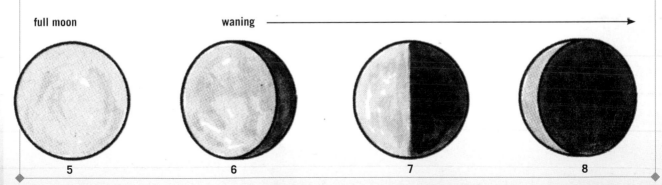

full moon   waning ⟶

5   6   7   8

Moth Watch

Magical Granny, now is your chance to wow your grandchild with your ability to predict an eruption of moths. It's simple. A couple of days before your night foray, mix your bait, allow it to sit and ferment, then paint your lure together.

MOTH BROTH

Ripe banana
Brown sugar
Stale beer or active dry yeast and warm water
Other ripe fruit such as pears, peaches, plums, and watermelons (optional)
1-inch paintbrush

Your grandchild will be a perfect fruit squisher. Let him go to it. Stir the fruit and the other ingredients together for a thin paste, and let it sit for a couple of days. (I store it in the warm garage and cover it with screening to keep flies away.)

In the late afternoon before your night explorations, paint a broad swath (about 12 inches by 12 inches) of moth sauce on chosen tree trunks or fence posts at a child's eye level. Be careful not to spill the sauce on the ground or you'll attract ants.

The best moth-watching hours are on warm nights between 10 p.m. and midnight. Wake your grandchild, pick up your flashlights or headlamps and magnifying glasses, and trek outdoors together for a moonlit adventure. Make a point of explaining that you'll need to sneak up on the moths as quietly as possible or they'll take flight. The "ear" (tympanum) of a moth picks up the sounds you make and quickly sends it a warning.

The temptation is great, but don't shine your flashlight on the trunk until you are right beside it, then remove the cellophane and flick it on. You will be rewarded with dozens of moths of various shapes, colors, and sizes with eyes that glow like brilliant red and orange coals.

THINGS TO OBSERVE:

Look closely at the moth's head and its long tongue-like proboscis that probes at the sauce and sips it through two fused, strawlike tubes. When the moth stops sipping, the tube will recoil like a spring and disappear below the head. Moths have combed, tapered, or feathered antennae that receive scents, such as a female's pheromones, that waft through the night air for miles. The sensitive antennae also sense sweet aromas that signal a nectar-rich meal. If you gently touch a moth's scaly wings, you'll see a light powder on your fingertips. The powder is the residue of the tiny scales that give each species of moth its signature pattern and color. Entomologists believe that the slippery powder may help a moth free itself from a spider's sticky web.

The proboscis of a sphinx moth may be longer than its body.

BAT ATTITUDE: STOP, LOOK, AND LISTEN

Find an area outdoors that is brightly lit at night. Streetlights, store windows, security lights, and athletic fields are just a few of the places to try. Sit quietly nearby and watch for moths and bugs that are attracted to the light. Soon, if you're lucky, a bat might swoop past and eat his supper on the wing. Bats can eat hundreds and sometimes thousands of insects a night! Watch moths dive to try to escape the bats.

Luna moth

Polyphemus moth

These moths feed voraciously in their caterpillar stage, but once they emerge from their cocoons, they just search for mates.

JEWELS OF THE NIGHT

Did you know that meteors may appear in a variety of colors? I've seen them glow deep emerald green, ruby red, pumpkin, golden yellow, or blue. Usually this occurs during the Perseids and Leonids.

Shooting Stars

Children are so used to being told to go to bed that it is a rare turn of events when, in the middle of the night, their granny wakes them and invites them to go outdoors for an adventure. Surely, only a magical granny could predict one of the most wondrous and memorable sights ever—a star-flecked sky pierced and scribbled with streaks of shooting stars.

Rouse your child between the hours of midnight and dawn, grab a flashlight and some blankets, and head outdoors to a dark area far from street or porch lights. If there is a moon, situate yourselves with the moon behind you. Stretch out on your backs on one of the blankets, wrap up in the other, and watch and wait (you won't have to wait long). You may see dozens, sometimes hundreds, of Mother Nature's fireworks on a good viewing night.

August, summer vacation time when a grandchild is likely to visit, is the month for the most brilliant displays of meteor showers, called the Perseids. If you trace their trails backward, they appear to be streaking out of the constellation Perseus. The Perseids occur on August 12, but usually you can see star shower activity six days before the projected date and three days afterward.

While you're waiting, tell your child a story (you're not teaching, you're sharing) about these sparkling pieces of heaven. The stellar fireworks, which most of us call shooting stars, are tiny particles of interplanetary rocks, ice, and dust—galactic rubble or debris formed from a disintegrating comet. The comet debris, heated by the atmospheric friction of the journey, ignites, glows, and vaporizes as it zooms through the inky sky. Some night you may be surprised and shocked by a fireball (called a bolide), such as one my son and I saw as it streaked across the black sky. The fireball, which was as bright as a flash of lightning, lit up the ocean and coastline so clearly that we could see a distant point of land and the outlines of faraway sand dunes. Some fireballs sport long, luminous trains of rainbow-colored vapors that remain visible after the fireball disappears.

METEOR SHOWERS TIMETABLE

Here are the best times to watch the nighttime lightshows. Mark your calendar in case a little one is visiting.

★ January 3: Quadrantids

★ April 22: Lyrids
   April 23: Pi-Puppids

★ May 3: Eta-Aquarids

★ August 12: Perseids

★ October 10: Draconids
   October 22: Orionids

★ November 13: Leonids

★ December 6: Phoenicids
   December 14: Geminids
   December 23: Ursids

Around the Campfire

Close your eyes and remember how magical it felt to be huddled around the campfire when you were a child. You toasted marshmallows and listened to the haunting hoot owls and the eerie fingernails-scratching-a-chalkboard *screeeee* of barn owls. You told scary stories and dumb jokes, sang songs and played music, and burned your tongue on hot s'mores. Nothing has changed. It is still magical, still enchanting, and still fun. It seems like the more complex and electronic our lives are, the more important such simple pleasures and immediate, natural experiences become.

Some of the best times with my grandchildren are when we are huddled around the fire in our backyard. Often, we construct story chains, beginning with a few sentences such as, "When I lived on a tiny island and I was rowing to shore, I dropped my oars and began to float out to sea." Then we move around the circle, each of us adding our own colorful embroideries to the story. Wow, you'll be amazed how a child can relate a story when given the chance in the limelight!

Take time to sit together around a campfire and talk, but, more important, *listen*. Share snippets of family history,

Everything is more magical by firelight.

transport your grandchild to new vistas and experiences, and let her transport you to a different viewpoint on life. Oh, and don't forget to toast those marshmallows or make some s'mores (see recipe, right).

CAMPFIRE STORIES

Sit and listen to the night sounds and see how many you can identify. Whoever names the most gets to pick the topic. To get you started, here are a few subjects that have generated some of our best talks:

- What was the funniest thing that you ever heard or saw?

- If you had only one wish, what would it be?

- Tell me about your best-ever outdoor adventure.

- Tell me about a place you've visited out of town.

- What is your favorite song? Can you sing some of it?

- What is your favorite animal and why? What interesting facts do you know about it?

- Who has done something kind for you? What did they do? What kindness have you passed on to others?

- Weave a story around where you want to go on vacation and what your adventure will be when you get there.

- Name two things you love and tell a story about them.

RECIPE FOR S'MORES

In case you've forgotten this iconic campfire treat:

Ingredients
Chocolate bar
Graham crackers
Marshmallows
Peanut butter (optional)

Put a piece of chocolate on top of a graham cracker square.

Toast a marshmallow until golden brown. Place the hot marshmallow on top of chocolate and top with another graham cracker.

"Cooking is at once child's play and adult joy.
And cooking done with care is an act of love."

CRAIG CLAIBORNE

CHAPTER THREE

KIDS IN THE KITCHEN

Sometimes when I walk into my kitchen and smell the scents of baking or a soup simmering on the old stove, memories rise inside me like the clouds of meringue on my grandmother's Heavenly Pie. I'm a child again, and I can close my eyes and see myself ensconced on a stool in my grandma's joyful kitchen. She prided herself on the shelves of "put by" food and the ability to make a great meal out of whatever was at hand, with enough left over to share with an unexpected guest.

My grandmother's well-scrubbed and organized domain turned into pure chaos whenever I arrived to "help" cook. She never minded the mess or scolded me when I stuck my thumb through an egg and dropped bits of shell into the batter. What I most remember about our cooking together is that we laughed, tasted, licked spoons and bowls, and then dug our fingers into the sides of freshly iced cakes as if we were both five and being naughty together.

COOKING UP A FAMILY TRADITION

One of the most joyous discoveries of my life came when I unpacked a box in my mother's garage and found over a hundred years of precious family recipes. I use those proven winners often, and I am saving them in a family scrapbook to pass on to my grandchildren.

Whenever you cook together and find a recipe you love or one you've concocted on your own, keep a record of it. Start a little card file or fill a family scrapbook with photos of you and your grandchild in the kitchen, and jot down recipes, shortcuts, and your own cooking tips. Your youngster will love looking through this record, and someday your collection will be a family heirloom.

Along the way, I learned the basics of making orange marmalade, scrambling the perfect egg, rolling a pie crust (albeit patchy), and an array of other accomplishments. I got acquainted with herbs, dried and candied our homegrown figs, and dodged the eccentricities of frightening pressure cookers, which always seemed ready to explode.

When my grandchildren ventured into the kitchen and began to work with me, I felt the tug of the invisible thread of continuity. No matter what disaster occurred, we adjusted and worked through the mess. No matter what flopped, flipped, dribbled, splattered, or sprayed, we triumphed, and because the kids weren't taken to task for minor problems, every experience gave them more self-confidence and skill.

For this chapter, I chose an array of simple comfort-food recipes to make with and for your grandchildren. Some of them were family favorites, but all of them are definitely granny-style, kid-friendly, fun, quirky, and downright memorable. What child wouldn't love cookie-cutter animal farm pancakes, beans in a blanket, or bird nests filled with tiny candy eggs?

PREP SCHOOL

Before your grandchild arrives, stock an easy-to-access (kid height) drawer or shelf with an array of child-sized tools, an apron, oven mitts, and mini cupcake liners. Include an assortment of toppings, such as dragees and sprinkles in a multitude of shapes—hearts, stars, and animals. Buy whimsical pastas, like animals or letters of the alphabet. I guarantee that when you unveil these tools and treats your young chef will be ready to roll up his sleeves and get busy.

SHOPPING

Introduce your grandchild to your local farmers market. It is beautiful and lively, and it connects children to the farmers or gardeners who grow great produce. It also educates them about good, healthy food, where it comes from, and how it is grown. They will learn that, if the produce is organic, it is safe, tasty, filled with nutrients, and good for them.

Before you go to the grocery store or farmers market, sit down at your kitchen table and get your grandchild's thoughts about what foods are favorites and what would be fun to cook. Pick a meal you would like to make together and list the ingredients you'll need.

At the market, let your child be part of the process of choosing. Examine produce and ask how the fruit or veggies look. Point out things that are right or wrong with the food and how to tell if something is ripe, check expiration dates, and don't be afraid to ask questions of the growers.

When you return home, put away the groceries and wash the produce together. These seemingly mundane chores can be interesting for a child who is happy just to be working alongside you. At the same time, he will become familiar with stocking a kitchen and preparing for cooking.

POWER-PACKED

A recent study published by Newcastle University, European Union, found that organic wheat, tomatoes, lettuce, and cabbage have up to 40 percent more essential vitamins and minerals than conventionally grown crops.

OUTFITTING THE LITTLE CHEF

Preparing for "Restaurant Night at Home."

Here are some simple things you can do to make your grandchild's cooking experiences safe, fun, and easy.

★ Provide your grandchild with an apron. All kids love wearing them.

★ Tuck a hand towel into the chef's waistband for easy cleanup.

★ Arrange a work area that is scaled to your child's height. Use only a child-safe stepstool (available online and in cooking and toy stores).

★ Cover the table with newspaper or a spill-resistant tablecloth or painter's drop cloth.

★ Keep a basket, box, or drawer filled with child-friendly kitchen items, like a small spatula, whisk, rolling pin, cookie cutters (without handles) for pancakes and potatoes, pizza wheel, blunt kitchen shears, muffin tins, cake pans, measuring cups, measuring spoons, unbreakable mixing bowls, bread knife for spreading and cutting soft foods, and small cooking pots.

★ Use a safe, handheld immersion blender—it's lightweight and saves on cleanup because you blend in the same container you use for preparing. My granddaughter calls the blender "the magic wand" because of all the amazing tasks it accomplishes.

★ Many cooking projects can be done in a portable electric frying pan or a small toaster oven set on the worktable. Explain that these appliances should never be touched or used unless you are in the room.

Home, Safe Home

Before you begin cooking together, talk about basic kitchen safety. Explain that a child can't use knives without supervision or turn on appliances or a stove without Granny nearby. And always follow these safety measures:

1. Wash hands with warm, soapy water before doing any prep work and after handling meats, raw eggs, or unwashed fruits or vegetables.

2. Roll up sleeves or wear short sleeves to prevent accidents.

3. Band or tie long hair so that it doesn't interfere with cooking or vision.

Keep a supply of child-sized cooking tools, pans, and bowls on hand.

Let your grandchild do any necessary measuring, both with spoons and cups. Teach your helper how to do a level spoonful by using a knife edge to scrape extra ingredients off the top of the cup or spoon. This experience is a great math lesson and helps develop coordination and self-confidence.

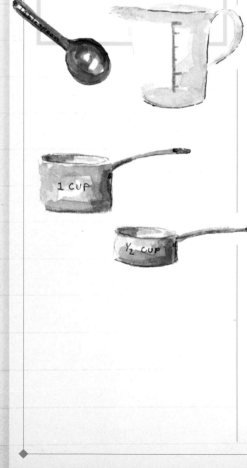

EVERYTHING IN ITS PLACE

To cut down on the time it takes for a youngster to do the hands-on work of cooking, I prechop items and have them lined up on the worktable ready for little fingers. As a child gets older and has better motor skills, these tasks will be safer and come more easily. Choose easy recipes to cook together and don't expect your youngster to help you cook an entire meal. One project, such as scrambled eggs, may be all that a child can handle. And that's a big accomplishment! Before you start, make sure everything is "at the ready."

★ Clear your work area.

★ Read the recipe out loud.

★ Check the recipe to see if you need to preheat the oven. If so, do it now.

★ Ask your grandchild to help you locate the ingredients in a recipe and move them to your setup area. Some of the items may be too high or out of reach, but you can find them and pass them to your helper.

★ Take out measuring cups, spoons, sifters, and any other tools you'll be using.

★ Set up a line of bowls for each ingredient needed.

★ Measure ingredients and put them in the bowls in the order in which they will be used. Grown-up chefs refer to this time-saver as *mise-en-place*, which simply means "everything in its place." By teaching your grandchild this time-saving strategy, you've saved hours of time in his future kitchen.

BREAKFAST

Breakfast is my family's favorite meal, and why not? Fresh fruit, drifts of airy scrambled eggs, crunchy granny-ola, and pancakes—just thinking of these foods makes my mouth water. Set your table with real napkins, a small vase of flowers, good plates, and glasses. Take your time eating, talking, and celebrating the perfect beginning to a new day.

Slippery-Slider Smoothies

I've never met a child who doesn't love fresh fruit smoothies. They're a great breakfast substitute when your grandchild isn't in the mood for a full-on breakfast. They're quick, easy, and filled with vitamins, minerals, and antioxidants.

Makes 1 smoothie.

INGREDIENTS

¼ cup sliced banana (about half a banana)

¼ cup berries or chopped fruit such as pineapple, peaches, kiwi, or mango

½ cup low-fat vanilla yogurt or child's favorite flavor (plain can make smoothie sour), frozen yogurt, or frozen juice concentrate for thickeners

¼ cup skim milk, soy milk, rice milk, or apple juice

½ teaspoon pure vanilla extract (optional, but divine)

TOOLS

Measuring cups and spoons

Big bowl

Immersion blender

Toss the fruit into the bowl, and add the thickener of choice.

Put the immersion blender into the bowl, turn it on low. Then as your helper gets used to it, turn up the speed.

Turn off the blender, add the liquid (milk, soy, etc.) and the vanilla extract, and puree on high until the ingredients are combined and the smoothie is the consistency you want.

A Seussian Scramble

Most children are aficionados of the Dr. Seuss books, and this is a great way to entice them to cook their own version of green eggs and ham and get them to eat it, too. Read the story of *Green Eggs and Ham* aloud while your grandchild enjoys this breakfast (children of all ages love this book).

One of the first foods my granddaughter Sara May learned to make was perfectly scrambled eggs. The secrets to her success? A child-sized iron skillet, sweet butter, and the deft swirl of a kid-sized spatula.

Makes 1 serving.

INGREDIENTS

2 large eggs

Natural green food coloring (always use the natural, available at health food stores)

2 teaspoons butter

¼ cup ham or vegetarian ham

Tiny pinch of salt and pepper

TOOLS

Medium bowl

Whisk

Child-sized spatula

Small nonstick or seasoned frying pan

Show your grandchild how to give the side of an egg a good firm tap on a flat, hard surface (a countertop is perfect).

Hold the cracked egg and use two thumbs to open it and drop it into the bowl. If a piece of eggshell gets into the bowl, just use a large piece of eggshell to remove it.

Whisk the egg, and add a few drops of the natural food coloring. Keep whisking until the color is blended.

Place the frying pan on medium heat, and after half a minute, drop in the butter and spread it around the pan.

Drop small pieces of ham or vegetarian ham into the hot butter.

FROG ON A LILY PAD

Whenever I tired of scrambled eggs, my grandmother thrilled me with this simple, fun-to-create breakfast. Here it is in rebus form.

Give your grandchild some [butter], a [knife] and a slice of [bread]. Butter both sides of [bread]. Use a [biscuit cutter] or glass to cut a [hole] in the center of the [bread]. Heat a [frying pan] on medium. Drop in some [butter], lay the [bread] and the [cutout] in the pan, and fry them for a minute. Flip the [bread] over. Crack a large [egg] and gently slip it into the hole. Cook to desired doneness. Set the cutout (frog) on top of the fried egg, and serve immediately. Ribbit!

Slowly pour the eggs into the pan (away from the child), and let the mixture sit for 15 seconds.

Gently scrape the spatula across the bottom of the pan and away from the chef.

Scrape again, and stir until fluffy curds form.

Remove the pan from the stove, and immediately slip the green eggs onto your grandchild's plate. (If you leave eggs in pan, they will continue cooking and become rubbery.)

Critter Cakes

I'm crazy about cookie cutters, and I'm always looking for new and unusual shapes. My grandkids love them too, not only for cookies, but also for clay crafts and for making our custom pancakes. Use handleless cutters to make the filling and flipping easier for your child.

Make your pancake batter from scratch or from a good commercial mix. Whichever you do, keep your grandchild involved every step of the way, from measuring and mixing to ladling and flipping.

To help move the pancake process along, premake the dry ingredients, and store the mix in a glass jar with your grandchild's name on it. That way she can reach into the cupboard, pull out her own homemade mix, and add the rest of the ingredients.

GRANNY'S HOMEMADE PANCAKE MIX

7½ cups all-purpose or unbleached flour
¼ cup baking powder
1⅓ tablespoons salt
⅔ cup sugar

Stir all ingredients thoroughly. Store the mix in an airtight container in a cool place.

Makes 12 to 14 pancakes depending on the size of your cookie cutters.

INGREDIENTS

2½ cups homemade pancake mix (above)
2 large eggs
2 cups milk
½ stick butter, melted (warm, not hot), plus 1 tablespoon butter
3 teaspoons pure vanilla extract
Spray cooking oil
1 cup fresh or frozen berries (see Note)
Pure maple syrup

TOOLS

Big bowl
Small bowl
Whisk
Big wooden spoon
Small ladle
Animal cookie cutters
Frying pan (I love a seasoned iron skillet for this recipe)
Spatula (child sized)

Pour the homemade pancake mix into a big bowl.

Lightly whisk the eggs in a small bowl.

Add the milk to the eggs and whisk. Then slowly add the melted butter.

Add the vanilla to the egg mixture, and whisk.

Slowly add the moist ingredients to the dry mix, and stir just until combined. Don't overstir—a bit lumpy is fine! If batter is too thick, add water one teaspoon at a time.

Spray the inside of the cookie cutters with cooking oil.

Set the frying pan on high heat for about 1 minute, then turn the heat down to medium and wait another minute.

Cookie cutters make forming and flipping pancakes easy.

Place 1 tablespoon of the unsalted butter (or a tiny bit of cooking oil) in the pan.

Arrange the cookie cutters in the pan—don't crowd them. Let your helper use the ladle to half fill each cookie cutter with batter. Don't fill to the top, as the batter will double and overflow. (I love the careful ladling done by my grandchildren, who fill every nook and stop at just the right time.)

As the pancakes cook, ask your grandchild to look for the tiny craters that will form on the pancakes, signaling that it's time to flip them.

Quickly slide a spatula under each cookie cutter and flip it. Cook for another 1 to 2 minutes.

Remove pancakes from cutters. Serve hot, or keep a single layer of the pancakes on a cookie sheet in a 200-degree oven till ready to serve. Sooner is better than later.

Note: Some people like to mix berries or cut fruit into the pancakes, but my grandkids like the berries over the top. I mix a couple of cups of fresh berries with a cup of pure maple syrup and heat it slightly. Yummy!

Fluffy Clouds

We call our flamboyant breakfast extravaganza "Fluffy Clouds." Other cooks know them as "Dutch Babies," but whatever you call them, they're delicious. The clouds are easy to make and beautifully fluffy when you remove them from the oven. There is something quirky about these that children love. Let your granchild sift a "snowstorm" of powdered sugar over the top.

Makes 4 to 6 clouds.

INGREDIENTS

6 large eggs, room temperature

1½ cups milk, room temperature

1 cup bread flour, sifted (which gives you the most puff for your buck)

3 tablespoons granulated sugar

1 teaspoon pure vanilla extract

½ teaspoon ground cinnamon

6 tablespoons butter, melted

1 teaspoon lemon zest

Confectioners' sugar for dusting the clouds

A LITTLE DAB'LL DO YA

Whenever my grandmother and I baked together, I was in charge of measuring and adding the vanilla—my favorite ingredient—to the recipe. Before she put the bottle of vanilla back into the cooling cupboard, she always dabbed a little behind my ears and on my wrists for a sweet perfume—a tradition I carry on to this day.

TOOLS

Big bowl

Measuring cups and spoons

Sifter

Immersion blender

10- to 12-inch frying pan or a 9-by-13-inch baking pan
(about 2 to 3 inches deep)

Grater

Small bowls

Position a rack in the center of the oven, and preheat the oven to 425°F.

In a big bowl, beat the eggs until frothy and light. Slowly add the milk, sifted flour (this is a chore your grandchild will love), granulated sugar, vanilla, and cinnamon. Continue blending for about 1½ minutes.

Preheat your pan in the oven for a couple of minutes.

Pull out the oven rack, and pour the melted butter into the pan, making sure to cover the entire bottom of the pan.

Quickly pour the batter into the pan, and slide the rack into the oven. DON'T OPEN the oven door until your cloud has baked 25 minutes. Open and close the door gently or the cloud will flop.

Bake for 25 to 30 minutes, until the cloud rises and is a light golden color.

While the cloud is baking, finely grate the lemon zest into a small bowl.

Quickly but gently remove your cloud from the oven. Immediately have your grandchild dust the top with a sifting of confectioners' sugar and a sprinkling of lemon zest.

Serve hot with one of the toppings below.

CAN YOU TOP THIS?

While the clouds are baking, line up small bowls on the table and fill them with toppings such as berries, applesauce, sliced peaches, sliced bananas, and pecan pieces. Let your child choose and top with any or all.

Molly's Berry-Basket Biscuits

·····································

Years ago, I visited author Molly Chappellet at her home in the Napa Valley, and she shared this recipe. I love it because it not only involves your grandchild in the making of the biscuits, but also turns the process into an occasion for berry picking and picnicking. The biscuits are great to make when wild blackberries are in season. You can also use fresh strawberries, jam, or a frozen berry mixture that is heated.

Makes 4 to 6 large biscuits.

INGREDIENTS

2 cups sifted cake flour

2½ teaspoons baking powder

1 teaspoon salt

½ stick cold butter (the real stuff, never margarine)

¼ cup shortening, chilled

18 tablespoons buttermilk (This equals 1 cup plus 2 tablespoons, but children love counting, and counting this many tablespoons of buttermilk turns into fun for them.)

2 cups berries

Heavy cream (optional)

TOOLS

Sifter

Measuring cups and spoons

Big bowl

Two butter knives

Lightly floured breadboard

Biscuit cutter (2 inch) or a small glass

Cookie sheet, greased

Place a rack in middle of the oven. Preheat oven to 400°F.

Show your grandchild how to sift the dry ingredients together into a big bowl and then how to use two knives to cut cold butter and shortening into the dry ingredients. We call this method "lobstering," because it resembles the way a lobster uses its two front claws. Don't overwork it; the mixture should resemble small peas. Your grandchild should gradually add the 18 tablespoons of buttermilk while you stir the mixture gently until the dough is mixed through.

Turn your sticky dough onto your prepared breadboard. Quickly pat the dough into a round that is about ½ inch thick. (You could roll it, but a child will love the quick patting process.)

Cut the biscuits with the cutter (or a glass).

Place biscuits about 1 inch apart on a greased cookie sheet.

Bake until a soft, golden brown, about 10 to 12 minutes.

Let cool for 5 minutes. Slice the giant biscuits in half, scoop on the berries, and pour a thick coating of cream inside. Yum!

LUNCH

Ahhh lunch, time to pause together to refuel with simple foods and ideas for the rest of a busy day. Keep it simple and dip into some "Super Snacks" for extra go-power.

Heidi Sandwich

My early dislike of the taste and texture of cheese led to this simple sandwich, inspired by Johanna Spyri's book *Heidi*. Heidi lived in the Swiss Alps with her grandfather, who fed her thick crusts of bread with chunks of cheese toasted on an iron fork over an open fire. I tried my own version of this on a coat hanger when I was young, and managed to drop every bit of cheese into the fire before I could get it onto the bread. Thank goodness for broilers.

Warning: Please don't try this recipe in a microwave oven; the cheese turns into a sheet of rubber.

INGREDIENTS

Slices of hearty bread, such as sourdough or whole wheat

Butter, room temperature

Honey mustard (optional, but tasty)

A good melting cheese such as mozzarella, Muenster, Cheddar, Jarlsberg, fontina, Gruyère, or Monterey Jack, sliced

Grown-ups like the addition of grated Parmesan cheese

TOOLS

Bread knife

Cookie sheet

Grater

Set the broiler tray in the middle position and turn on the broiler.

Place the slices of bread on the cookie sheet. For special occasions (like Valentine's Day), I use big heart-shaped cookie cutters to make specially shaped Heidis.

Let your grandchild spread the soft butter onto the bread.

Slide the buttered bread under the broiler, and cook for about 1 minute.

Move the cookie sheet to your work area. (The cookie sheet is HOT, so use caution.) Let your helper place thin slices of the cheese onto the bread until it is completely covered. Spread with a little honey mustard if you like.

Slide the cookie sheet under the broiler, keep the oven door ajar so you can watch, and broil for about 2 minutes or until cheese starts to bubble.

Open the broiler, sprinkle a bit of the Parmesan over the bubbling cheese, and cook for about 30 seconds with the door ajar again. Grandma should remove the Heidis from the cookie sheet. Serve hot with a bowl of tomato soup or the Alphabet Soup on the next page.

Alphabet Soup

When I serve alphabet soup, it sometimes gets cold before my grandkids get around to sipping it. They love to fish through the broth and lift out letters to spell their names or their friends' names or special words they are studying in school. They're so entranced by the soup they actually eat the veggies without even knowing it.

Since you'll be working with a big pot of HOT ingredients, spend your time together preparing and measuring everything, setting up the ingredients, and setting the table. Teach your helper never to reach over a hot pot or to touch the stove top.

Serves 4.

INGREDIENTS

1 cup sliced carrots

½ cup sliced celery

1 cup diced onion

1 tablespoon olive oil

1 tablespoon butter

2 cloves garlic

1 cup fresh spinach leaves

1 one-quart box vegetable, chicken, or beef broth

1 cup water

½ cup alphabet pasta

1 teaspoon dried oregano or mixed Italian herbs

Salt and pepper

Parmesan cheese, grated (optional)

TOOLS

Cutting board

Knife (grown-up does the cutting)

Measuring cups and spoons

Big soup pot or Dutch oven

Granny does the prep work for this recipe since it involves a lot of knife work. You'll need to slice carrots into thin coins, slice the celery, and dice the onion. Turn on the burner under the soup pot. Add the olive oil and the butter and stir. Add the carrots, celery, and onion to the pot.

Then, your grandchild can help:

Whack the garlic cloves with a can, roll the can over the cloves to moosh them, peel off the skins, and toss the cloves into the pot.

Tear the spinach into small pieces.

Add the broth and water to the soup pot. Turn burner heat to medium and cook the soup (without a lid) for about 10 minutes.

Add the alphabet pasta and the torn spinach, and cook another 8 minutes.

Season with oregano or Italian seasoning.

Add salt and pepper to taste.

When serving, top with a light dusting of Parmesan cheese, if desired.

Simple Summer Berry Soup

Who knew you could make a fruit soup? And eat it cold? You and your grandchild can change the star of this soup depending on what fruit is in season. I've used blueberries fresh from the woods, luscious strawberries, and peaches. Whatever you choose, it will be delicious.

Makes 4 small servings.

INGREDIENTS

1½ cups cream (you may substitute soy milk or rice milk)

1½ cups orange juice

½ cup yogurt

1 tablespoon sugar or honey

1½ cups fresh or frozen berries

Chunks of fresh fruit, for topping

Ground nutmeg or cinnamon, for topping

TOOLS

Big bowl

Immersion blender

Ladle

Small bowls

Pour ingredients (except toppings) into a big bowl.

Blend with the immersion blender until items are thoroughly combined, with no lumps remaining. The soup will be the glorious color of your fruit.

Chill in the refrigerator for about 2 hours.

Serve in individual bowls, topped with chunks of fruit dusted with nutmeg or cinnamon.

WASH, DON'T POLISH

All fruits and veggies must be washed before they're eaten. Polishing them on your jeans' leg just doesn't do the job! The agricultural and environmental scientists at Tennessee State University recommend that cooks cut off both the stem and blossom end of the fruit. Mix 3 parts of water with 1 part of white vinegar in a clean spray bottle. Drench produce with the vinegar spray, and then rinse under running water. Fruits and veggies that are not smooth (like cauliflower, broccoli, etc.) may need to be soaked in the vinegar water, then rinsed.

PLEASE PLAY WITH YOUR FOOD

Sometimes the best munchies are the unplanned kind, where you and your grandchild pick some things from the garden or pluck them from your refrigerator and assemble them into snacks and, believe it or not, food art. The simple act of working together to create food that is sculptural, pictorial, funny, and tasty is an unforgettable experience for a child.

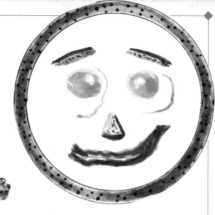

Plate face with toast eyebrows and nose, egg eyes, and bacon mouth

INGREDIENTS
Fresh vegetables and fruits
Cream cheese (to use as glue)

TOOLS
Bamboo skewers
Toothpicks
Paring knife
Small cookie cutters
    to cut shapes out of melons

Broccoli poodle

Caterpillar assembled from sliced cucumbers and carrot coins with celery antennae

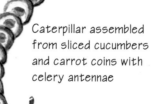
Partially peeled eggplant penguin

Green onion squid

Two peapods grasshopper

Radish dog

Bell pepper basket

SUPER SNACKS

- Keep a supply of Popsicle sticks on hand, and encourage your grandchild to make fresh fruit "yummies" for snacks. Use whole strawberries, chunks of banana (which taste like ice cream when frozen), cubed peaches, peeled kiwi, whole apricots (pits removed), and cut mangos. Poke the Popsicle sticks into the fruit, immediately wrap them in plastic, and freeze. These "yummies" make a refreshing (and healthy) treat on a hot summer's day.

- I refused to eat celery when I was a kid, but when my grandmother stuffed it with peanut butter, dropped a few raisins on top, and called it "ants on a log," it was my favorite snack. Simple, healthy, and fun—just what kids want.

- Combine 2 or 3 cups of Granny-ola (see page 112) with more dried fruits, carob chips (these taste and look like chocolate), some salty pretzels and nuts, sesame sticks, and soy nuts. Mix them together and package them in snack-sized bags to carry along on your outdoor explorations.

- Grape marbles are one of my favorite hot-weather snacks. Bite into them and they explode with a juicy, refreshing flavor. Freeze whole bunches of grapes (don't worry about wrapping them). Use them as a snack or as a substitute for ice cubes in a fruity drink.

- Strawberry bugs are ALMOST too adorable to eat, but kids will enjoy devouring them, usually head first. Hull strawberries and poke a blueberry into the wide end with a short piece of toothpick to make the head. Use another toothpick to pierce the sides of the berry with six holes. Stick a tiny sliver of celery into each hole to make the legs.

- Hollow out the center of a cantaloupe, small watermelon, or honeydew melon and set aside. In a medium bowl, blend 1 cup of raspberry yogurt with ⅓ cup of soft cream cheese and 3 teaspoons of lemon juice. Stir in some frozen raspberries and chill. Fill the melon with the fruit mixture, and dip into it with fruit slices or carrot sticks.

- With a pizza wheel, cut a package of soft tortillas into pie-shaped wedges (stack the tortillas three deep to speed things up). Spread them in a single layer on a greased cookie sheet, and lightly spray with cooking oil. Bake wedges in a 350°F oven for 7 to 10 minutes (watch closely or they'll singe) until crispy. Remove chips from the oven and lightly dust them with cinnamon and sugar.

- Find the tiniest carrots available, clean them, and store them in a container in the refrigerator. Label the container FAERIE FINGERS, and watch how they disappear whenever it is snack time.

- Prepare popcorn, and store it in individual sealed sandwich-sized bags in your cupboard. Pull it out whenever your grandchild wants a quick bite to eat.

The Faeries' Tea Party

This may sound like a party for girls, but I've found that most little boys respond to the magic and mystery of tiny foods made by the faeries. I've included some of my menu favorites as a suggestion, but I encourage you to make up your own. Ask your grandchild for his ideas about what kinds of foods the faeries would eat, and then experiment together. Keep things simple and accessible, think small and whimsical, and then make your own variation of the faeries' picnic. This is a fun process, so enjoy every step.

Menu

Heart- and star-shaped faerie sandwiches

Apple slice sandwich

Fruit salad on a "twig"

Petite carrot pocket

Stuffed hollyhock blossoms

Button pie

Faerie punch

PREPARING FOR THE PARTY

Find a small basket, line it with a piece of fabric, tuck the picnic inside, and tie the fabric closed with a piece of ribbon. Stow the picnic basket and food in a cool place until you "discover" the gift from the faeries and go outside for a picnic.

THE SMALLER THE BETTER

Many cooking and specialty stores have child-sized baking supplies available. I love the tiniest muffin tins for faerie cakes and the miniature, ruffled candy cups, which can be used as cupcake holders.

hearts & stars

Remove the crusts from bread, and use a small heart- or star-shaped cookie cutter to create your sandwiches. You can fill the sandwiches with whatever your grandchild enjoys, but I like to spread a thin layer of sweet butter on the bread, sprinkle lightly with sugar, and top with a confetti of the colorful petals (always unsprayed flowers) of roses, violas, Johnny-jump-ups, carnations, dianthus, or lilacs.

apple sandwich

Thinly slice an apple and quickly dunk each piece into lemon juice to keep it from discoloring. Smear peanut butter on one slice and top with another.

fruit on a twig

Faeries love to eat their fruits fresh-picked and strung on a twig, but for safety's sake, your faerie fruit will be strung along pieces of uncooked spaghetti. Break the spaghetti into short sections and pierce the fruit, alternating among strawberries, melon, grapes, blueberries, and raspberries. Don't use bananas, which will quickly discolor.

petite carrot pocket

Find the tiniest carrots available. Fold a lettuce leaf inward to form a little pocket. Tuck in a line of baby carrots; tie the pouch closed with raffia or a strappy chive spear. Leave the little tips of the carrots showing at the top of the pocket.

hollyhock blossoms

You'll need a container of your grandchild's favorite flavored yogurt. Suspend a cheesecloth-lined strainer or colander over an open bowl in the refrigerator. Add yogurt and tiny pieces of raspberry, blueberry, strawberry, and pecans, and let it drip overnight or until it is firm. Stuff the cheese-like mixture into a washed hollyhock bloom (keep cool).

button pie

Buy a refrigerated, premade pie crust (okay, do it from scratch if you want), and unroll it onto a work surface. Use a small, round cookie or pastry cutter to create mini pie crusts. Crimp the edges lightly and sprinkle with cinnamon and sugar and transfer to a cookie sheet. Bake at suggested temperature, but check often as they burn quickly. Remove button pie crusts from the oven, let cool, and fill with fresh fruit or jam. Drop a dollop of whipped cream on top and finish with a tiny mint leaf.

faerie flower ice cubes

Fill an ice cube tray with hot water from the tap. Drop a small blossom of lilac, viola, borage, Johnny-jump-up, or rose petal into each section of the tray. Freeze. Make lemonade and add a blend of berries to give it zing. Drop in some flower ice cubes.

DINNER

I love sharing dinners with my grandchildren, and I try to make our meals special occasions. It gives us a chance to work together in the kitchen, set and decorate the table, light the candles, and hold hands and share why we are grateful. Oh, and let's not forget the most important part of a family meal: everybody talks and we always laugh a lot. Recently I learned that having breakfast for dinner is my grandchildren's favorite treat. For them, a serving of waffles, eggs, and other breakfast foods is better than going to the fanciest restaurant in town. See page 81 for some great kid-friendly breakfast recipes.

Beans in a Blanket

No matter how finicky my grandchildren are about food, there are certain things that are accepted without question, like these Beans in a Blanket. I don't know if they would like them as much if I referred to them as burritos, but "beans in a blanket" definitely wins them over. You and your grandchild can set up the ingredients and work assembly-line style at putting them together. Of course, this dish is also finger food, which seems to hold extra appeal for the under-12 set.

Makes 4 to 6 tortillas.

INGREDIENTS

1 package tortillas (see Note, facing page)

1 cup Monterey Jack and Cheddar cheeses, grated together

3 tomatoes

1 head lettuce

1 can red kidney, black, or refried beans

1 jar salsa or mild taco sauce

TOOLS

Aluminum foil

Grater

Cutting board

Knife

Small bowls (five)

Small pan

Wrap the tortillas in aluminum foil and warm them in a 250°F oven while you prepare the ingredients. Supervise the grating of the cheeses while you dice the tomatoes and your helper tears the lettuce. Transfer the prepared vegetables and cheeses plus the salsa into individual bowls and line them up on the counter or table.

Place the beans in a pan and heat slowly over medium heat. Keep an eye on them because they burn quickly.

Remove the tortillas from the oven and set them on the cutting board or work space.

Supply your grandchild with leathery leaves to make place cards for the dinner table. Use acrylic paint or markers (you can buy silver and gold markers) to write the name of each person.

Remove the beans from the stove top, transfer them to a bowl, and place them near the toppings. Unwrap the foil and put a tortilla on a plate.

Spread beans on one side of the tortilla. Spoon lettuce, tomatoes, and cheese on top of the beans.

Roll the tortilla into a snake shape, and dot it with taco sauce. Repeat for the rest of the tortillas. Dig in!

Note: Many markets (especially health food stores) sell colorful tortillas made from spinach, tomatillos, squash, etc. These add even more lively color and nutrients to Beans in a Blanket.

Mac and Cheese Made with Ease

Is mac and cheese a phase that every child goes through? For a while, when one of my grandchildren visited, she would *only* eat mac and cheese. I've learned to always have the ingredients in my pantry. This make-and-serve version doesn't require any baking—which is great if you have a hungry child. Let your grandchild measure, grate, and whisk the ingredients.

Serves 4 to 6.

INGREDIENTS

2 teaspoons salt

½ pound dry elbow macaroni or any dry pasta in whimsical shapes, such as animals, stars, etc.

2 tablespoons unsalted butter

1½ tablespoons unbleached flour

1 cup milk

½ pound Cheddar cheese (you can mix in Monterey Jack cheese too)

½ cup grated Parmesan cheese

TOOLS

Large pot

Grater

Colander

Skillet

Whisk

Spoon

HIDDEN IN PLAIN SIGHT

The best way to slip vegetables under your grandchild's veggie radar is to give them center stage on your table. Clean and slice celery, red and yellow bell peppers, carrots, and tiny "trees" of broccoli. Tuck them into a small vase filled with cold water, and set them within reach of your grandchild. Fill small bowls with ranch or other favorite dressings and dip into them.

Start your pot for the macaroni with two quarts of water, add salt, and bring to a rolling boil. Add the macaroni to the boiling water and cook according to directions, usually 6 or 7 minutes. Stir occasionally. Don't overcook the pasta!

Pour the macaroni into a colander and drain it in your sink.

While the pasta coooks, prepare the cheese sauce. Put the skillet on medium heat, drop in the butter, and slowly sprinkle in the flour, whisking continually.

Add the milk and whisk constantly until the mixture thickens slightly.

Add the Cheddar cheese to the mixture and stir for a couple of minutes until cheese is melted.

Turn off the heat under the cheese sauce and move the skillet to a cool burner.

Add the macaroni to the cheese sauce, sprinkle with the Parmesan cheese, and stir.

Note: If you feel you *must* bake this, butter a 9-by-13-inch pan, pour in your mac and cheese, top with another half cup of grated Cheddar cheese, add some seasoned bread crumbs if you want a crunch. Bake for half an hour at 350°F.

THE POWER OF THE TABLE

Vanderbilt University professor David Dickinson and researchers from Harvard University studied why some children are able to read at an early age while others fall far behind. Their research indicated that shared mealtimes, where actual give-and-take conversations occur, are a strong predictor of how a child's language skills and literacy will develop. Question your grandchild about his day, empathize, keep a dictionary nearby to look up unusual words, and savor each other as well as your food.

RESTAURANT NIGHT AT HOME

Whenever you suggest something unexpected and out of the ordinary, you can count on your grandchild's eager participation. Restaurant night at home will stir up a whirlwind of ideas. Think of the possibilities: hand-decorated menus, custom-made place mats, the chance for *you* to be served by your grandchild, and memories that will last a lifetime.

- Set aside some time to figure out a simple, easy menu for an Italian spaghetti dinner. Print it legibly for your grandchild, and supply him with paper, markers, and whatever is necessary to hand-make menus for everyone.
- Scan or copy the tricolored Italian flag, and print out copies to be used as place mats.
- Open a full-sized sheet of newspaper, and cut a head-sized hole at the fold to make a drip-stopping spaghetti bib. Set the table with candles, a bouquet, real dishes and wineglasses, which you can fill with sparkling water or fruit juice, and big (preferably checkered) napkins.
- Play Italian music.
- Show your grandchild how to serve food to the guests. Drape a towel over his arm, carry dishes to each person, and unfurl napkins onto the diners' laps.
- Buy fresh Parmesan cheese and let your grandchild grate it onto each person's plate of spaghetti.

Even a simple grating job will give your grand a sense of accomplishment.

SPAGHETTI DINNER

Roasted Tomato Sauce

Yummy roasted vegetable tomato sauce will be easy for you and your grandchild to prepare and won't entail the use of big, heavy pots. Most of your time will be spent carefully chopping the ingredients, which, when roasted, are rich, complex, and incredibly tasty. You can make this sauce the day before Restaurant Night and reheat it as your pasta is cooking. The flavor just gets better the second time around.

Enough for 1 pound of spaghetti.

INGREDIENTS

Extra-virgin olive oil to coat the baking sheet and drizzle on
    veggies
2 onions
1 head garlic, separated into cloves and peeled
2 stalks celery
2 carrots
2 pounds fresh Roma tomatoes (about 16 tomatoes),
    cut into chunks (see page 157 for growing your own)
1 can (28 ounce) of crushed whole tomatoes
    (Italian Romas have more taste)
Fresh or dried parsley, oregano, and rosemary to be sprinkled
    over the top of the sauce
Sea salt and pepper to taste

TOOLS

Baking sheet
    (unlike a cookie sheet, this has rolled sides)
Knives
Big bowl
Spatula
Immersion blender

Preheat the oven to 425°F.

Prepare the baking sheet with a drizzle of the olive oil.

Set up a workstation at your child's height and allow your helper to cut alongside you with a serrated bread knife (firm tomatoes are easy for them to cut in halves and quarters).

Cut the fresh vegetables into small chunks so they cook uniformly, and toss them into the bowl.

Drizzle the vegetables with the olive oil and sprinkle them with about 2 teaspoons of sea salt. Then show your grandchild how to use his hands to toss and mix the veggies until they are thoroughly coated with oil and salt.

Help your grandchild transfer the vegetables onto the baking sheet in a single layer. Don't crowd them or they'll steam rather than roast.

Roast for 15 minutes, then stir and flip the vegetables.

Roast for another 15 minutes and stir vegetables again. Spoon the crushed tomatoes over the vegetables.

Your helper can sprinkle oregano, rosemary, and parsley over the vegetables.

Continue roasting for another 15 minutes.

Remove from the oven and transfer the vegetables to the big bowl.

Use the immersion blender to mix the vegetables into a saucelike consistency. Season to taste.

Spaghetti

....

If you grew a spaghetti squash (page 157) or found one at your market, now is the time to bake it. Preheat oven to 375°F and show your helper how to poke holes in the skin with a sharp fork or paring knife, so the steam can vent. Roast for about 1½ hours. Remove squash from the oven, cut it in half, and scoop out the seeds. Use your "lobstering" technique with two forks to lift the strands out of the squash. Drizzle the spaghetti squash with olive oil or butter and top with sauce.

If you're making store-bought pasta:

Serves 6 to 8.

INGREDIENTS
2 quarts cold water
2 teaspoons sea salt
1 pound spaghetti
Fresh Parmesan cheese
Roasted Tomato Sauce (facing page)

TOOLS
Large pot
Big wooden spoon
Grater
Colander

In a large pot, bring the cold water to a rolling boil, add the salt, and stir.

Holding the spaghetti in your hand, run it through cold water, then slowly add it to the boiling water. Stir for a minute and cook according to the directions on the package.

To taste for doneness—and the grandkids will love this—remove a couple of strands of spaghetti from the boiling water with a long wooden spoon, and toss it at a kitchen cabinet door. If it sticks, it's done.

Your grandchild can grate the Parmesan cheese while you finish the spaghetti.

Drain the spaghetti in a colander in the sink, but first reserve a couple of tablespoons of the good, thick cooking water and add it to the sauce for flavor. Quickly transfer your cooked spaghetti to a warm serving bowl, pour on enough sauce to coat the noodles, and toss. Add more sauce, if needed, or put the remaining sauce in a gravy boat or bowl for diners to serve themselves.

Yum. Everything is cooked; the kitchen smells great; the windows are steamed up.

Now you can light the candles, sit down, and enjoy a great Italian restaurant-at-home. And don't forget the wonderful grandchild servers. Tips are in order!

TIMING IS EVERYTHING

Fresh and dried pasta have differing cooking times. Check the package directions, but usually dried pasta takes at least twice as long to cook as fresh.

COMPOSITION IN LETTUCE

My grandmothers never heard me say, "Please pass the salad." A chunk of pale, tasteless iceberg lettuce dolloped with Thousand Island dressing was what I accepted as salad. Just as an iceberg sank the *Titanic*, so iceberg sank my interest in salads. It wasn't until college, when I began to study the history of gardens, that I learned it was once common for a "sallet" to contain up to 35 ingredients—none of them lackluster and tasteless like my old nemesis.

Take a walk with your grandchild through the produce department of a grocery store or a farmers market, and look at the varieties of lettuce and fresh greens that are available. The colors, textures, and tastes are amazing. Arugula has a rich nutty or peppery taste, sweet mâche melts in your mouth, kale crunches and has a bit of a bite to it, young leaves of deer tongue taste buttery and mild—the choices are endless! So no excuse, step up to the produce with your tote bags and buy something that is new to you. Try different, tasty dressings your grandchild might enjoy, like ranch or homemade honey mustard. Once you and your grandchild start composing beautiful salads together, you'll never be satisfied with boring iceberg again.

A few packets of seeds (the last great bargain) yielded this container of lettuces, herbs, and edible flowers.

A KIDS' SALAD BAR PARTY

Throw a Salad Bar Party for grandkids and their friends, family, and neighbors. Encourage your guests to bring along a favorite lettuce, fruit, or veggie topping or dressing. Set up your serving table a few hours before your guests arrive, and decorate it with a big "bouquet" of cabbage or lettuce and assorted vegetables. Wait until the last minute to set out your serving bowls of ingredients.

★ Cover your dining table with brown kraft wrapping paper instead of a traditional tablecloth. Provide small buckets or terra-cotta pots of crayons for each grandchild and friend. Ask them to do their best artistry on the paper and to sign each work. You'll be amazed by what they'll create.

★ Premake a few unusual salads to set the tone. Form a cup of lettuce leaves to resemble a nest, trim it with sprouts, and nestle some radishes inside. Cut a red or yellow bell pepper into horizontal rings and stick endive or romaine inside the ring for a "stand-up" salad.

★ I'll bet you'll be able to entice even the most vegetable-challenged children to partake in the offerings of a salad bar if they're allowed to make their own choices, construct their own work of edible art, and fill their plates with whatever they want.

Hands-on is always the best teacher.

★ Offer at least six different kinds of greens and cabbage or kale. Set up a separate bowl for each variety and provide serving forks or tongs.

★ Mound an array of ingredients and toppings (see suggestions on the next page) in little bowls and on platters, and provide spoons for serving.

- ★ Offer a variety of salad dressings, from creamy French and ranch to homemade oil and vinegar, in easy-to-pour containers.
- ★ Stack salad bowls, forks, and napkins at one end of the table.

IDEAS FOR SALAD BAR INGREDIENTS

- ❀ Greens of all kinds
- ❀ Sprouts
- ❀ Veggies such as carrots, celery, pieces of broccoli, scallions, edamame
- ❀ Fruits, such as tomatoes, avocados, dried cranberries, apple slices, raspberries, grapes
- ❀ Nut toppings (Make sure to label them in case any of your guests have allergies.)
- ❀ Grated, cubed, and sliced cheeses
- ❀ A few herbs that go great with greens, such as basil, chives, cilantro, and dill
- ❀ Edible flowers (see page 163)
- ❀ Croutons (make your own, see right)
- ❀ Sea salt (fine grain)
- ❀ Pepper

Edible flowers add color, taste, and zing to your salads.

Croutons: No Squares Allowed

Tiny cookie cutters are perfect for making a child's version of croutons. Use a dense day-old bread or sourdough for best results.

Preheat the oven to 350°F.

Spread unsalted butter on both sides of the bread.

Cut out a variety of whimsical shapes.

Heat a skillet on low, and add two parts unsalted butter to one part olive oil.

Gently drop the tiny cutouts into the skillet, stir, flip, and toss till coated.

Spread the croutons on a cookie sheet, put in oven, and bake until golden.

SPIN-OFF

A big THANK YOU to the inventor of the salad spinner. I used to wash all my greens, tie them in a clean pillowcase, and tumble them on the cool setting of my dryer, but now I am saved by this wonderful kitchen tool. When we have greens to prepare, my grandchildren do the rinsing and spinning, which is one of their all-time favorite jobs.

DESSERTS

As far as my grandchildren are concerned (and probably yours, too), dessert should be served first. Although they may be "too full to eat another bite," somehow there is always room for dessert. I'll admit that I am a bit lax when it comes to enforcing the rules about cleaning a plate before the grand finale. I figure I feed them veggies and fruits during the day. Reality can set back in when they return home—I exercise my grandmotherly privilege of treating them to uncommon delights when they visit.

Great-Granny Aggie's Peanut Butter Cookies

My granddaughter Sara May announced one afternoon that she wanted to bake something. We didn't have much time left together and so I turned to the four-ingredient peanut butter cookie recipe shared with me by Great-Granny Aggie Goettie. This recipe couldn't be simpler, and Sara crowed with pride when she read the recipe and did everything (except removing the hot cookie sheet from the oven) on her own. In less than half an hour, we had three dozen small peanut butter cookies cooling on a wire rack.

Sara's description of them—"Perfect, crunchy, better than peanut butter candies."

Makes 36 small cookies.

INGREDIENTS

1 teaspoon baking soda

1 cup sugar

1 cup peanut butter (we love crunchy, but you might prefer smooth)

1 large egg, lightly beaten

TOOLS

Medium bowl

Teaspoon

Big bowl

Wooden spoon

Small whisk

Tablespoon

Cookie sheet, greased with spray oil

Fork

2 small bowls

Spatula

Cooling rack

Preheat the oven to 325°F.

In a medium bowl, let your grandchild stir together the baking soda and sugar.

In a big bowl, mix the peanut butter and dry ingredients. Your helper can lightly beat an egg in a small bowl, and then add it to the peanut butter mixture. Stir the cookie dough until it is blended.

Use a tablespoon to drop the peanut butter mixture onto the greased cookie sheet (leave about 1½ inches between).

Show your helper how to dip a fork into a bowl of water and make a criss-cross pattern on top of each cookie.

Bake for 10 to 12 minutes. Transfer the cookies to a rack to cool.

These chewy nests are easy for the youngest chefs to make.

4 cups cornflakes
¼ cup toasted coconut
Candy eggs

Nonie Clarke's No-Bake Nests

These feather-light cookies are not only tasty, but also beautiful and whimsical. I am on the lookout year-round for candies that look like eggs. During holidays and summer, I find candy eggs that are blue with speckles, and I sometimes use the traditional wedding favor eggs, almonds coated in pastel colored sugar. When I make little hummingbird nests, I use tiny jelly beans.

Makes 36 nests.

TOOLS
Large saucepan
Measuring cups and spoons
Big spoon
Teaspoon
Muffin pan
Baking sheet covered with waxed paper or parchment

INGREDIENTS
34 large marshmallows
½ cup unsalted butter
1 teaspoon pure vanilla

In a large saucepan, stir the marshmallows and the butter together over medium heat.

Add the vanilla to the melted marshmallow mixture and stir. Remove from heat.

Fold in the cornflakes and the lightly toasted coconut, and mix.

Drop 1 teaspoonful of the mixture into each cup of a greased muffin pan. Show your grandchild how to form a small nest by carefully sticking thumbs into the ball and pinching gently around the edges to make a cup shape.

Remove once they're formed and place on a baking sheet. Nestle a pair of small, colored candy eggs inside each one.

Cover with plastic wrap and let harden overnight on the countertop.

Store nests in a single layer in a tightly covered container.

Gramma Gimmy's Mini Mug Cake

....

This child-friendly recipe was given to me by my dear pal Mary Rae Means, aka Gramma Gimmy. The treat is a favorite not only for little kids, but also for the big ones who flock around their own mugs of this rich and easy minicake.

Yields 1 12-ounce mug or 2 servings.

INGREDIENTS

4 tablespoons flour

4 tablespoons sugar

2 tablespoons unsweetened cocoa powder

1 large egg, beaten

3 tablespoons milk

3 tablespoons walnut or coconut oil

½ teaspoon pure vanilla extract

3 tablespoons chocolate chips (optional)

Vanilla ice cream, to top

TOOLS

Measuring spoons

Small bowl

Tablespoon

Medium bowl

Fork

Large microwavable mug (about 12 ounces)

Let your grandchild dump the flour, sugar, and cocoa into a small bowl and stir to mix well. Next, mix the egg, milk, oil, vanilla, and chocolate chips (if used) in a medium bowl.

Fold the dry ingredients into the liquid, add chips and mix thoroughly.

Pour the chocolate mixture into a microwave-safe mug.

Microwave on high for 3 minutes. The ingredients will rise up and double in size like a soufflé, but they won't spill over the edge of the mug.

Use pot holders to carefully remove the hot mug from microwave. Scoop it out into two bowls and top it with vanilla ice cream. Dig in.

Cindy Rankin's Dump Cake

This scrumptious cake is the simplest one you will ever bake. I turn to it whenever my grandchildren are in the mood for baking—and you will too. They'll only need to "dump" ingredients into the cake pan.

Makes 12 servings.

INGREDIENTS

1 can crushed pineapple, with juice
1 can cherry pie filling
    (or other pie filling, if you prefer)
1 box yellow cake mix
1½ sticks unsalted butter, melted
1 cup pecan pieces, sliced almonds,
    or walnuts, finely chopped
Whipped cream

TOOLS

9-by-13-inch cake pan
Big spoon

Preheat the oven to 375°F (350°F if you're baking in a glass pan).

Have kids pour the undrained pineapple and pie filling into the pan and mix with spoon.

Sprinkle the yellow cake mix evenly over the fruit layer.

Drizzle the melted butter over the top of the cake mix, making sure to drizzle along the edges to keep the cake from sticking while baking. Sprinkle the nuts over the top.

Bake for 30 to 35 minutes. The cake is done when the edges pull away from the sides of the pan and are slightly crisp.

Remove the cake from the oven and cool on a rack for about 20 minutes.

Serve warm, topped with whipped cream.

Variation: You can substitute an apple pie filling, and a spice cake mix for the yellow mix. It's a yummy choice for an autumn meal.

LET THEM EAT COLOR

When my grandson Asher turned five, we worked together on a boxed yellow cake for his birthday. Although he loved doing the mixing, he wasn't happy with the "boring color." He wanted green, his all-time favorite. So now whenever we whip up a cake together for a birthday, the honored grandchild chooses his or her favorite color for the frosting *and* the cake.

FLAVORED SUGARS

PETAL POWER

Pour a thin layer of sugar into a jar. Have your grandchild add a thin layer of fragrant (unsprayed) rose petals on top of the sugar. Repeat this process until the jar is full of alternating layers. Store covered and use for cooking and teas.

VANILLA SUGAR

Slice a vanilla bean down the center, cut it into short lengths, and bury the pieces in a jar of sugar. Store with the lid on, and when you need a special sugar for cooking or tea, it will be ready.

LAVENDER OR ROSE SUGAR

Pour a handful of dried lavender or rose blossoms into a blender or food processor and pulse them until they are powdery. Add the flower powder to a jar of sugar and shake to blend. This sugar is excellent for custards and ice creams.

SCENTED LEAF SUGAR

Many of the scented pelargoniums (called geraniums) have aromatic leaves that lend themselves to cooking. In a jar, alternate layers of fresh leaves with sugar. Cap tightly.

JAPANESE *KYARABEN*

Japanese children carry their lunches to school in a small, compartmentalized container called a bento box. Portions of rice, fish, fruit, noodles, and vegetables, just the right size for finicky eaters, are tucked into each section. Nowadays, the bento box lunches have turned into works of art. Parents interested in getting their youngsters to eat an array of healthy offerings arrange them into compositions called *kyaraben* or *charaben,* which means "character food."

Their food creations include animals, characters from cartoons, movies, and television, musical instruments, landscapes, houses, cars, portraits, insects, and the alphabet—the only limit is imagination. Practice doing fun food projects with your grandchild. You don't need to buy a bento box; just do it on a plate or platter and enjoy every minute of creating it.

Molded rice head, carrot ears, tangerine nose, lettuce leaves hat and collar, red pepper lips, half apple cheeks, and celery whiskers.

THE SUNSHINE KITCHEN
Making a Solar Oven

What could be more earth and child friendly than cooking in a Sunshine Kitchen? No worry about hot electrical elements, no gas or propane, no charcoal, wood, or matches, no fancy equipment—just a bright, sunny day and a few hours of play or patience. You and your grandchild will be rewarded with a great meal you created together in harmony with nature. What better way to teach her about the endless possibilities of harnessing solar power?

WHERE AND WHEN TO COOK

The optimum time to cook is on bright, clear, sunny days between the hours of 8 a.m. and 3 p.m. Choose a flat, sunny area that is protected from the wind, face the open solar oven toward the sun, and keep the shadow of the lid behind the food. To "preheat," set your oven in the sunshine about a half hour before placing food inside. As the sun moves through the sky, you may have to move your cooker slightly to keep the box and lid in full sun. Food cooked in a solar oven is heated from the top down, the opposite of how our indoor ovens work, and it takes twice as long.

Don't worry about overcooking; just put your food in the cooker in the morning and leave it till late afternoon.

Pizza Box Oven

Save that used corrugated cardboard pizza box to make your own solar oven. You'll be able to sun-dry fruits and tomatoes, and make campfire-style s'mores, melted cheese sandwiches, nachos, English muffin mini pizzas, cookies, biscuits, and other baked treats. This oven should heat to about 275°F on a sunny day.

YOU'LL NEED:

A sheet of acrylic glass or Plexiglas, slightly smaller than the lid but bigger than the flap you'll be cutting. You can find these in hardware stores, craft stores, and home improvement stores.

Pizza box of corrugated cardboard (use the largest pizza box for a bigger cooking area)

Marker pen

Ruler

Box cutter (Granny should do the cutting)

Heavy-duty aluminum foil

Scissors

Glue

Black construction paper from a craft or art store

Duct tape

Nail

String

1. Center your sheet of plastic on the lid of the box and trace its outline on the box with a marker.

2. Remove the plastic and draw another outline about 1 inch inside the first.

3. Use the box cutter to cut three sides of the inner line. Leave the back side (nearest the hinge) uncut.

4. Lift the cut portion and crease along the uncut line to form a flap.

5. Close the flap and open the box lid to expose the inside.

6. Cut a piece of aluminum foil to the exact size of the inside bottom of the box, and glue it in place.

7. Tape a piece of heavy black paper over the foil to absorb the heat.

8. Cut another piece of aluminum foil to the size of the flap.

9. Carefully glue the foil to the underside of the flap and press it smooth. When foil is wrinkled, the reflected light bounces off in many directions.

HOT

flap

10. Open the box lid, place the plastic on the underside of the lid, covering the flap opening, and tape it to the lid along all four sides. This helps retain the heat.

plastic top

11. Poke a nail into the back side of the oven. Tape one end of the string to the top edge of the flap. Open the flap and run the other end of the string around the nail. Use the string to adjust the angle of the flap to catch the sun's rays. Tie the string to the protruding nail.

RECIPES

Moon Pizzas

My granddaughter Sara looked at her first English muffin and immediately identified it as a moon. The name stuck, and now our simple little solar pizzas are always called moons.

INGREDIENTS
English muffins
Olive oil
A jar of pizza sauce
Shredded cheeses
Toppings, such as diced pineapples
    and sliced bell peppers

TOOLS
A dark cookie sheet to fit inside the pizza box oven
Tablespoon

Split the moon-shaped muffins apart and place them on the cookie sheet. Drizzle on a small amount of olive oil. Spread 1 tablespoon of pizza sauce onto each muffin. Sprinkle shredded cheeses across the top of the pizza sauce and finish them with the toppings of your choice.

Set the cookie sheet inside the pizza box oven. Close the oven lid. Situate the flap so that the sun hits the muffins.

Bake till the cheeses are melted.

Moon pizzas can bake while your grandchild plays outdoors.

TEMPERATURE TRACKER

Keep an oven thermometer in your pizza box oven so you can track the temperature. Note that when you lift the lid, the temperature can quickly drop by as much as 50 degrees.

Granny-ola

What could be better for breakfast than a crunchy bowl of cereal baked in your own solar oven? I've tasted lots of store-bought mixtures, but nothing rivals homemade. I think the children in your life will agree. Jazz up the Granny-ola by adding dried fruit toppings or by mixing it with flavored yogurt instead of milk.

Makes 4 servings.

INGREDIENTS

4 tablespoons vegetable oil

4 tablespoons honey or maple syrup

1 teaspoon pure vanilla extract

1 cup old-fashioned, rolled oats

½ cup sliced almonds

¼ cup light brown sugar, firmly packed

¼ teaspoon salt

½ teaspoon cinnamon powder

½ cup dried apple pieces, cranberries, or raisins

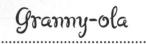

TOOLS

Measuring cups and spoons

Small bowl

Big spoon

Plastic wrap

Big bowl

Dark cookie sheet (must be dark so
        it will absorb heat)

Spatula

Pour vegetable oil, honey or syrup, and vanilla into the small bowl and stir gently. Cover the bowl tightly with plastic wrap and set it in the sun until ingredients warm.

Mix oats, almonds, brown sugar, salt, cinnamon, and dried fruit in the big bowl. Pour the warm oil, honey, and vanilla over your mixture and stir with a big spoon till well mixed.

Spoon a thin layer (thick layers won't bake) of the mixture onto the dark cookie sheet. Slip the cookie sheet into the pizza box oven. Close the window lid. Face the oven toward the sun. After 2 hours, stir and turn the ingredients with the spatula to toast evenly. Cover with lid and continue baking. You can't overcook this mix.

Remove from the oven, cool, and store in a container with a tight-fitting lid.

Half-Baked Apples

Grandmother Lovejoy was passionate about cooked apples, and she passed that passion on to me. For this recipe, you will want to use tart, firm cooking apples, such as Rome Beauty, Gala, Fuji, Jonagold, McIntosh, Pippin, Northern Spy, Granny Smith, or Winesap. This treat is great topped with a dollop of ice cream or whipped cream.

INGREDIENTS

¾ cup light brown sugar

1 teaspoon cinnamon

1 teaspoon pure vanilla extract

½ cup chopped pecans and/or raisins

2 apples

1 tablespoon butter

TOOLS

Medium bowl

Dark cookie sheet

Melon scooper

Teaspoon

Pour ½ cup sugar into the bowl. Add the cinnamon, vanilla, and chopped nuts or raisins. Your grandchild can finger-mix the ingredients together.

Cut the apples in half so that they will fit into your pizza oven when the lid is closed. Use a melon scooper to remove the core and seeds, but don't poke through the skin or the filling and juices will drain out.

Fill the center of each apple half with the mixture. Top the filled apples with a small pat of butter, and sprinkle some of the remaining brown sugar over them.

Bake in your pizza box oven till the apple is soft and the brown sugar has formed a crunchy crust.

Susan Branch's Banana Bliss

The first time Sue served me bananas baked in their skins I couldn't believe my taste buds. The heavenly texture, aroma, and taste of a baked banana is indescribable. When the bananas are thoroughly baked, they'll turn black, which signals pure perfection. Kids will be delighted at how good the "burnt" bananas taste.

INGREDIENTS

Ripe yellow (not black or green) bananas

Vanilla ice cream

Sprinkles, chopped nuts, and/or chocolate chips

TOOLS

Dark cookie sheet

Oven mitt

Preheat your solar oven and lay your unpeeled bananas onto the cookie sheet.

Bananas should bake until they turn black, about half an hour. Remove them, slit the skin (take care, they'll be hot), spoon on some ice cream, and add the toppings of your choice.

"Tell me and I'll forget;
Show me and I may remember;
Involve me and I'll understand."

CHINESE PROVERB

KITCHEN GARBAGE GARDEN

Learning from Leftovers

My grandmother's kitchen was not just a kitchen—it was a science lab, greenhouse, herb room, bakery, confectioner's workshop, art studio, and much more. The kitchen was the soul of my grandmother's house where magic happened every day with commonplace ingredients. Carrot top forests sprouted on the sunny windowsills. Avocado pits suspended by toothpicks over water struck out tentative roots, then split and pushed their green shoots into view. Sweet potato vines sitting in old canning jars of water looped around windows and scrambled across the top of the refrigerator and into the pantry. In spring, egg cartons of tomato seedlings, whose seeds were saved from our salads, thrived in the breakfast nook, and spindly grapefruit, lemon, and orange trees, started from seed in old tin cans, poked through the soil and leaned toward the light.

Grandmother and I tried to grow everything. Some seeds and cuttings were a heart-lifting success, others didn't work, but for me, the thrill was in the experiment. I found it amazing that something normally overlooked or thrown away could be coaxed into life. If a plant failed to thrive, no problem! It became part of the cycle of life. From the kitchen to the compost pile, back into the garden, and maybe, somewhere down the line, into the kitchen again, where the whole experiment could start over.

Now it is your turn to introduce your grandchild to the simple joy of growing plants from leftovers. You'll open little eyes to the miracle, something I call the "possibility factor," that is inside every seed, root, cutting, and pit. You may not harvest peanuts or a pineapple this time around, but you will share the wonder and excitement that happens when a child realizes that with just a bit of love, water, and light, he can coax life from the most unlikely scraps.

Part of the joy of these projects is that they're done indoors, which is perfect for grandmothers who live in an apartment, condo, or townhome. You and your grandchild will be in close daily contact with the "friends" that the plants become, and can easily tend them and watch their daily progress. The magic of life will unfold right on your windowsill or kitchen table.

Tomato seedlings are nursed along in recycled citrus shells, then transplanted to recycled containers.

SIMPLE ESSENTIALS

Scout your house for anything that can be used as a container for your indoor garden. Use old milk jugs, fruit juice bottles, yogurt and cottage cheese containers, egg cartons, empty rinds of oranges and grapefruits, wooden boxes, canning jars, big coffee or tomato cans, trays, crockery—any container that will hold soil. Remember to poke holes in the bottom for drainage.

TUCK saucers and trays underneath your plants so that overflows don't damage your furniture. Saucers should be filled with an inch of gravel or pebbles. Pour water into the gravel until almost covered. This will provide humidity for your garbage plants, but not let them become waterlogged.

KEEP a cup of old cutlery, some chopsticks, and a pencil near your indoor garden to use as handy work tools. Till the soil with a fork and turn the soil with a spoon. Use a knife to lift plants, and a pencil or chopsticks to poke planting holes into the soil.

RECYCLE a spray bottle, clean it thoroughly, and fill it with water. Let the kids mist the plants in their garbage garden daily. The spray will keep plants moist and helps to discourage some pesky pests such as spider mites. Your grandchild will LOVE doing this.

STOW a magnifying glass near your garbage garden so kids can be detectives. If a plant shows signs of illness or wilts even though it has been watered, have them pull out their magnifier and look closely at the tops and undersides of the leaves for signs of insects.

Gently clean a parsnip, turnip, daikon radish, and any other root veggies or members of the onion family that you want to include in this project. Select some jars or glasses tall enough to hold the veggies' crowns above the water level. Slide the vegetables into the containers and set them in a brightly lit area. Wait and watch! Change the water every day to keep it clear.

TLC FOR YOUR PLANTS

Your indoor garbage garden plants need to be lightly fed once they begin to grow. Treat them monthly to a dose of natural fertilizer, which will slowly release nutrients to the growing plants.

Your garbage garden plants will thrive in a sunny southern window or under artificial lighting such as a Gro-Light. An architect's lamp, shown here, with a common incandescent bulb of 60 to 100 watts works well, but situate it at least 30 inches above the plants. Fluorescent tubes or bulbs provide great lighting and should be hung about 20 inches above your plants. HID bulbs, which have three times the output of fluorescent lights, will furnish enough lumens to satisfy a grouping of your light-loving garbage garden plants.

A leek, beet, kohlrabi, carrots, garlic, sweet potato, and a radish thrive on a kitchen windowsill.

GREAT GARBAGE GARDEN PLANTS

Below are a few of the easiest plants for your kitchen adventures, but don't be afraid to try anything. Think of each project as a challenge. Some of them may fail, but you'll learn something about each seed and plant and what they need to stay alive.

BEANS

The bulging bag of 15-bean soup sat on the counter and awaited its watery fate. I picked it up, showed it to my granddaughter, and said, "We can cook it all for soup, OR we can rescue a few of them and plant them in our garbage garden."

"Rescue," Sara said, and so we did. She poured out a handful and dropped them into a bowl of water. The floaters were losers, no longer viable for planting but fine for soup. The sinkers still had plenty of life left inside them, enough to burst into green finery in just a few days.

Sara pulled her wooden stool up to the sink, filled the colander with the beans we were going to plant, and ran a stream of warm water over them. The project was already a success as far as she was concerned. Whenever children get to puddle around in water, whether it is from a faucet, a hose, or a watering can, the water part is the thing that most enthralls them.

I pried her away from the sink and covered the farm table with newspaper so she could work with the beans and the soil. I handed her some spoons, and she shoveled the soil into yogurt containers, pushed too many beans deeply (too deeply) into them, and doused them with warm water. Instead of correcting the planting depth or the number of beans she planted, I let it go

A handful of dried soup beans quickly turns into a lush indoor garden.

Sara's Bean Soup Garden

till she left for the day. What could be more discouraging for a child than to have their work undone as soon as it is finished?

Sara watered her beans daily and on the fifth morning she discovered little curls of green popping through the soil. "I'm a bean mother!" she shouted joyfully.

BEAN WISDOM

Soak your beans to ensure that they are still viable. Like Sara, your grandchild will love this job. Poke drainage holes in the bottom of a recycled pudding, yogurt, or cottage cheese container and fill it with bagged potting soil. Show your child how to tuck the plump beans about 1 inch into the soil and have her water thoroughly. Then let her do the rest. Set the pot on a saucer or a tray filled with gravel and add water to the top of the gravel to ensure that your future crop has plenty of humidity. Set the future bean vines in a brightly lit area or a sunny window. Oh, and don't forget to add your child's homemade plant labels (see sidebar, page 122)—it's so easy to lose track of what is planted where.

Part of the joy of gardening indoors is the daily, intimate contact with the plants. Kids can check on them whenever they visit, water them when the top inch of soil is dry, and note on a calendar or in a journal when the first green shoots appear.

The extras that didn't make it into the indoor bean soup garden were planted outdoors.

BEAN TEPEES

Once the beans have grown three pairs of leaves, you can transplant them into a larger container that has a drainage hole. Lay a piece of nylon or screen over the hole, and then fill the pot with bagged potting soil. Because your beans want something to climb, poke five stakes (at least 18 inches tall) into the soil around the edge of the container. (You can use twigs from the backyard or buy bamboo stakes at a nursery.) Tie the stakes together at the top to form a mini tepee. Plant some of your bean sprouts at the base of each stake, and they'll twine their way to the top. Others will spill over the side of the container and form a curtain of greenery.

PUMPKINS

Sometimes carving pumpkins on Halloween caused some contradictory feelings in my grandchildren. We were happy for the fun we had making goofy-looking faces, but sad because we knew that by the end of the night the pumpkin would be a goner, partially collapsed from the heat of the candle and destined for the compost heap the next day.

To alleviate pumpkin anxiety, we rescued their seeds and tried to grow them indoors, and the experiment was a success. First, we sprouted some in paper towels and others in cups, then we planted the sprouted seeds in pots and let the vines meander freely over our table.

PUMPKIN PARENTING

Use ice cream scoops to dig out the seeds inside the Halloween pumpkins. Run water over the seeds, moosh them around in a colander or sieve, and spread them in a single layer on paper towels to dry.

After starting our pumpkin seeds in paper cups, we transplanted them into recycled pots.

WINDOW PEEPER

Glue a few pumpkin seeds onto half of a paper towel. Allow the glue to dry, then wet the paper towel and fold it in half. Slip the towel into a plastic sandwich bag and tape the bag to a window. Your grandchild will be able to watch the seeds sprout and begin to grow.

Sometimes it is hard to remember which things you've planted, so labels are a must. Have an art day at the kitchen table. Let your child use acrylic paint or markers on rocks, Popsicle sticks, or tongue depressors (now sold in craft stores as "craft sticks") to label each variety of seed planted.

Fill a 4- to 6-inch-wide container (don't forget the drainage holes) with bagged potting soil. Mound the soil in the center of your pot. Plant a couple of seeds about 1½ inches deep and water gently. Set the pot under a Gro-Light, Vita-Lite, or a bright incandescent bulb, or in a sunny, warm area such as a south- or west-facing window. They'll do best with ten hours of light a day.

Feed your hungry pumpkins with a weak or half solution of natural fertilizer every couple of weeks. Pumpkins are greedy eaters. Some people treat their pumpkins like babies and give them an occasional drink of milk.

Soon your pumpkins will thrust out their prickly stems and leaves. When the flowers appear, your grandchild will need to play the role of a bee and become a human pollinator. Male and female flowers will be on the same vine; the male flowers have a cargo of golden pollen (find the pollen grains with your magnifying glass), and the female flower has a round caboose behind the blossom. Have your child use a cotton swab or paintbrush to lift some of the pollen from the male, and transfer it to the open bloom of the female. Within days, the fruit of the pumpkins will begin to fatten. Because you want to concentrate growth in only one or two pumpkins per vine, pinch off other female flowers before they begin to grow.

CITRUS TREES

I remember sitting in Grandmother's cozy breakfast nook and wrestling with a half grapefruit full of slippery seeds. They were bitter, and they made it difficult to get a good bite of pure fruit without their unwelcome taste.

I didn't understand why these little inconveniences were necessary until the day Grandmother put a coffee can full of soil on the table in front of me, pointed to the seeds, and said, "We're going to grow a tree." Who was she trying to fool? I knew there was no way that a tree would grow from a tiny thing that was normally dumped into the garbage.

I spit a few of the slimy seeds into the old enamel colander, rinsed them under a stream of water, and nudged the seeds into the moist soil. Every day we checked on them, watered them when the soil was dry, and looked for a sign of life. In a few weeks, I had three tiny grapefruit trees poking through the soil. Two of the trees rotted, but one remained and grew and grew until it was about 2 feet tall.

SPIT AND SAVE

Have your child save some seeds from an orange or from any member of the citrus family. Rinse the seeds and soak them in a cup of warm water overnight. Fill a pot or recycled container (4 inches wide) with bagged potting soil.

Plant the soaked seeds two to a container and about ½ inch deep, and be sure to label them.

Water thoroughly and set the containers in a tray or saucer filled with some gravel and water.

Place the tray in a sunny spot.

Teach your child how to do the soil test by poking his finger down about 1 inch into the soil to see if it is moist. He should do this every few days to make sure the soil is still wet. When it is dry, it's time to water.

Once the seedlings sprout, make a point of checking their growth and health, and measure the trees monthly. Jot the growth in a journal or onto a kitchen garden calendar.

This citrus was started from a seed many years ago and now is a part of our family.

COMFORT ZONE

Plants won't flourish if they're in front of a heater vent or an air conditioner. Keep them away from drafts and set your thermostat between 65 and 68 degrees.

PEANUTS

Sara splits open a peanut shell and picks out whole peanuts to plant in a bowl filled with moist white yarn.

Warning: Children with peanut allergies should not attempt to grow these.

Although they're called peanuts, they aren't nuts; they're legumes and related to peas and beans. Unlike nuts, they don't have a hard shell but a soft one called a pod. The peanut doesn't grow above the ground; it develops underground in the darkness and cover of the soil. Peanuts are so easy to grow that even the jays that frequent my garden plant them successfully. Sometimes when I walk outdoors, it seems as though they're trying to turn my yard into a peanut farm.

I grew my first peanut plants indoors in a small plastic container filled with loosely packed white yarn. After it grew about one month, I transferred the peanut plant to a hanging container filled with bagged potting soil mixed with sand. Within days, the peanut flaunted new oval leaves and looked as imposing as the finest plants in my indoor garden. None of my visitors could believe that my beautiful plant was a common peanut, the same one used to make their favorite spread, peanut butter.

UNDERGROUND MAGIC

To help your child watch the underground magic happen, fill a fishbowl with pieces of light-colored yarn and wet it thoroughly. Have your grandchild open a peanut shell and pick out the two or three peanuts and drop them into the wet yarn. Cover the container of peanuts and yarn with plastic wrap and set it in a bright, warm spot. Lift the plastic wrap daily and check the yarn to make sure it is wet. You should see the peanut begin to root and grow within a few days. Remove the plastic after the peanut develops leaves and keep the yarn moist.

Three weeks after planting, the peanuts are flourishing and will soon flower.

HOMEMADE, HOMEGROWN PEANUT BUTTER

1½ cups of roasted peanuts mixed with about 1 tablespoon of peanut oil can be blended or mixed in a food processor to make a yummy butter. Add salt to taste. Store in the refrigerator for up to two weeks.

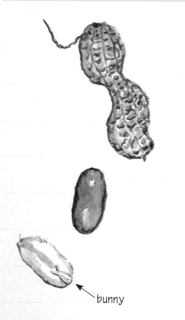

bunny

Carefully break a peanut in half and ask your grandchild to search for the tiny bunny hidden inside.

THE PEANUT GALLERY

You can also plant your peanuts directly into the soil. Poke drainage holes in the bottom of a large container that is at least 10 to 12 inches wide and add a 1-inch layer of gravel. Fill the pot with bagged soil mixed with sand. Pick out two or three peanuts from a peanut shell and tuck them into the soil about 1 or 2 inches deep and at least 3 inches apart.

Keep the soil moist, and set the container in a sunny or brightly lit, warm area with southern or western exposure. Don't forget to perch the pot atop a tray or saucer filled with gravel and water. Usually within a week, you'll see the buds and leaves poking through the ground. Water as needed and turn the peanut plant daily so that it doesn't lean toward the sun.

Peanut flowers open at night, are self-fertilized before sunrise, and shrivel by the afternoon. You and your youngster will need to look for the small, pealike, yellow blossoms early each morning before they begin to fade or use a flashlight to check on them during the night. Point out how the small leaflets fold together in pairs so that the plant appears to be sleeping.

Once your peanut flowers wilt, they will fall off, and a tiny shoot will grow toward the soil. After the shoot, which is called a peg, enters the soil, it will turn sideways and begin to form a peanut shell. A few weeks after the blooms nestle into the soil, let your child reach gently into the ground to check on the peanut's progress. Although your youngster may not stay with you long enough to harvest the peanuts, you can take a picture of the plant as you pull it, and send your grandchild his very own homegrown peanuts.

SPROUTING SPUDS

My grandchildren and I think it is miraculous that you can take a couple of pounds of potatoes, cut them into pieces (making sure there is an eye in each piece), and turn them into hundreds of potatoes. That's enough potatoes to make potato soup, scalloped potatoes, roasted potatoes, baked potatoes, french fries, and more. Only 2 pounds of potatoes can turn into over 50 pounds of food.

If you open your cupboard and find that, YIKES, some form of alien being has sprouted and is sending tentacles out into the world, you're lucky. You've found potatoes that may be past their prime for cooking, but they're ready to be planted. Don't waste them; use them as seed potatoes and plant them.

This sprouted potato is no good for cooking, but it can be cut into small pieces and planted.

SPUD STARTERS

I like to use organically grown potatoes, especially when children are handling them, because potatoes are one of the most heavily sprayed crops.

Involve younger kids who can't safely handle a knife by showing them how to locate the eyes, and then let them circle the eye with a marking pen. Granny should cut the potatoes into 1½-inch pieces that contain at least one, but preferably two eyes.

Let your child fill a tall container with drainage holes (gallon milk jugs or juice containers work well) with bagged potting soil, and tuck the small pieces or sprouts into the soil about 2 inches deep with the eye facing up. To help you both remember, just say, "Eyes to the sky." Cover the potato pieces with soil and water them. Set the container in a sunny area, and water only when the top inch of soil dries out.

Check every day for the first signs of green. Once the potato breaks through the soil, it quickly becomes a sprawling and exuberant kitchen plant starred with pale bluish-purple flowers that were once used to decorate lady's hats.

POTATO HEAD PORTRAIT

Select a firm potato and cut off one end to provide a flat base. With a melon ball scooper, lift out a bit of the potato's top to form a slight hole.

Use acrylic paint or food-grade paint or markers (commonly stocked in craft stores) to give the potato a face. Some children love to do family portraits. Use toothpicks to attach raisin eyes, circles of red bell pepper for a mouth, cauliflower florets for little ears—you get the picture.

Fill the hole at the top of the potato with a wet cotton ball.

Sprinkle the wheat berries (see page 132) onto the cotton ball and press them slightly.

Set the potato on a saucer and water daily. Within a few days, the potato head portrait will sprout bright green hair.

Note: If you want to transplant your potatoes and grow them outdoors, see the directions in "Kids in the Garden" chapter, page 139.

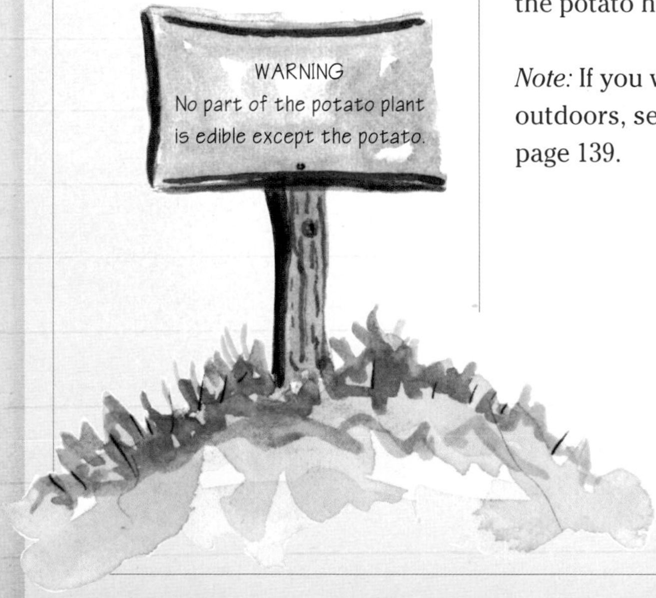

WARNING
No part of the potato plant is edible except the potato.

Potatoes-
Buried
Treasures

SWEET POTATOES

Grandmother Lovejoy's kitchen and living room were always adorned with the trailing vines of sweet potatoes. Her luxuriant plants, which were sometimes 20 feet long, sprang from a variety of containers filled with water and a tangle of roots. One of her most famous vines began its travels in the kitchen and ended up on the far side of the living room after traversing bookcases, a buffet, windowsills, and a mantel.

Sweet potatoes, which aren't true potatoes, are the thickened roots of a tropical vine related to morning glories. They're one of the first things I tried to grow indoors, and they were so successful that I once had three or four growing at a time.

TRAVELS WITH 'TATERS

Take your child to your local farmers market or grocery store to choose a firm sweet potato. Just in case the sweet potato has been treated with a growth inhibitor, scrub the skin gently with a vegetable brush.

Poke three or four toothpicks into the bottom third (pointed end) of the vegetable, and suspend it over a jar. Fill the jar with water until the bottom of the tuber sits in the water.

I've started the tubers in a brightly lit and a dark area, and each worked equally well.

Check the tuber daily to make sure that the water doesn't evaporate. Soon a few thin white roots will appear, and within days the jar will be crowded with roots and the sweet potato crowned with a stubble of green. Keep a tape measure close by to measure and record growth in a journal.

If the sweet potato's water becomes murky and a bit stinky, you'll need to give it a totally fresh drink. Help your child set the container in the sink directly under the faucet. Turn the cool water on low and run it into the jar until the water is clear.

A narrow-mouthed jar or forcing vase makes a great "starter home" for an exuberant sweet potato vine.

PINEAPPLE

PINEAPPLES AND PINECONES

Imagine what fruit-starved Christopher Columbus and his crew felt in the second discovery voyage of 1493 when they bit into their first tasty pineapple. They loved it, but what could they call this strangest of strange specimens? Anyone who has seen a whole pineapple will understand how it earned its name *piña* for its resemblance to a pinecone.

As a child, I only knew pineapple from a can. When I finally tasted fresh pineapple, newly sliced from an enormous, prickly specimen, well, I thought I had just bitten into a slice of Heaven. It's easy to understand why the pineapple is sometimes referred to as the princess of fruits.

Mother Nature is so amazing; I still can't believe that we can eat a fresh pineapple until there is nothing left but its crown of stiff spines, which we can plant and grow into another elegant pineapple plant. It wasn't until my friend Lee Taylor, a professor emeritus in horticulture at Michigan State University, explained the only "sure" way to get a crown to take root that I was able to grow one. His method is different from what most books describe, but if you follow Lee's lead (below), your child will be successful every time.

Cruise the fruit section of your grocery store and select two firm, fresh pineapples—one as an insurance policy and teaching (and eating) tool, the other for actual hands-on planting. Hold the "princess" in your hands and give the fruit the sniff test. A mature pineapple should have a mouthwateringly sweet fragrance, be a rich golden color, and a leaf should pull out easily.

LEE'S TWIST AND YANK

Contrary to what you'll hear, pineapple crowns *shouldn't be cut off* the top of the fruit. Set your pineapple on a table at child height, and use your extra pineapple as a visual aid. Show your helper how to grasp the base of the crown, and then twist it quickly, and yank off the top. You'll end up with a tuft of stiff leaves atop a pointed nub of yellow pineapple flesh. Pull off any flesh to prevent rotting, and tug off three or four leaves from the bottom. Use a sharp knife to make some thin, horizontal cuts in the stem until you see a circle of little brown spots, which will someday be roots. Stop cutting! Set the pineapple aside for a couple of days to dry, then put it into a jar of water until roots develop.

Choose a large, porous (to prevent rot) terra-cotta container at least 8 inches wide, and 7 to 8 inches deep for your pineapple's first pot, pour in a layer of gravel, and fill with bagged potting soil. Let your grandchild set the rooted pineapple crown in the middle of the container, brush soil around the base until the fruit nub and roots are covered, and water it until liquid starts draining from the bottom of the pot.

Set the pot on a saucer filled with gravel and ½ inch of water. Place the pineapple in a warm, sunny room with a temperature of 60 degrees and above. Make a ritual of checking the pineapple together to look for growth. Have your grandchild stick a finger into the soil, and if it is dry, water until the excess drains through and into the saucer of gravel.

This isn't a plant that will flower and produce fruit in a short period of time. A big part of the joy of this project is the anticipation of life to come and the miracle that from a stiff bristle of leaves an exotic and beautiful plant will be born and will be a part of your family for many years. If you keep your pineapple watered, fed, and in a warm and sunny spot, someday your child may discover spiky rosettes of pineapple bloom, and soon, some delicious, homegrown fruit.

Keep the base of the pineapple submerged and within a couple of weeks, threads of white roots will be visible.

WHEAT BERRIES

Until I saw a tray of vibrant green wheat growing like a mini lawn on a French tabletop, I considered wheat berries to be ingredients for baked goods, health drinks, or food for cats and dogs who love to graze on the tender stalks.

Because wheat berries are some of the speediest seeds to sprout indoors, they make an almost guaranteed-to-succeed project for even the youngest child. These seeds are a celebration of life, and they should be used frequently and in many different ways.

Select a shallow tray, plant saucer, or a plastic lidded container like the ones salad greens come in. Clean the container, and poke some drainage holes into the bottom, then fill it with an inch of soil, moss, or cotton batting.

Wet the planting surface thoroughly, scatter seeds across the top in a single layer, and cover with a thin layer of soil. Keep the medium moist, and the seeds will sprout in less than a week.

GROWING A NAME

Have your grandchild "write" his name in a tray of soil with a pencil or twig. Drop the wheat berry seeds inside the shallow pencil furrow, pat soil over the top, and water with a light sprinkling.

In just a few days, the child's name will erupt through the soil in thin green lines. Keep the sprouts watered and in a sunny spot, and the namesake display will last for weeks.

Note: You can trim the tops with scissors if the sprouts begin to droop.

A fresh tray of wheat berries will need a gentle sprinkle of water daily.

BEETS, CARROTS, LEEKS, AND GARLIC

One evening, my young son complained about us "hurting" carrots, leeks, garlic, and beets when we cooked them. I told him that we could choose a few for a reprieve, and that we would give them a second chance at life. Little did I know what a life lesson they would teach us.

Even without soil, these plants—kohlrabi, carrots, and garlic—will sprout and grow to amazing heights.

We picked out some firm beets that still sported their greens, a handful of carrots with tops, a plump head of garlic, and a pair of tall, fat leeks. We trimmed the tops off the veggies and slid them into some recycled milk jugs filled with bagged potting soil, and Noah gave them each a drink.

We were used to sprouting carrot tops on our windowsill—even that was miracle enough for us—but nothing prepared us for the surprise that these veggies provided. For the first few days after planting, they looked wilted and on their way to the worm bin. But after only a week, they began to flaunt their new green headdresses.

The beet greens flourished, the carrots looked like a feathery jungle, and the garlic produced an endless procession of tasty leaves that we continually cut and used in cooking, but the biggest surprise was the leek. It soared skyward and one day burst into a huge bloom that resembled Fourth of July fireworks. All this showy pizzazz from a few vegetables once destined for dinner.

PEEK-A-BOO PLANTERS

Find a clear plastic container (juice bottles work well once you snip off the neck) and poke drainage holes in the bottom. Fill with soil and set your planter in a pebble-filled saucer or plate to capture water overflow.

Wrap the container with black paper, and tape it closed so that no light can reach the soil. Plant your whole, firm vegetables in the soil close to the side of the peek-a-boo planter. Water gently. When the vegetables begin to sport new growth, lift the sleeve of paper and take a peek at the roots. See if you can spy on the underground happenings.

Note: You can trim your beet leaves and add them to a pot of steamed vegetables or soup. They're a tasty and healthful green. You may also want to transplant the beets outdoors if they outgrow their indoor garbage garden home.

GINGER HANDS

The next time you buy a fresh "hand" of ginger for cooking, pick up a couple of extras for your child to plant. Half fill a 6-inch-wide by 8-inch-deep pot with soil. Choose a "hand" that is about 3 inches long and have your child lay it horizontally (like it's taking a nap) on the soil. Top it with 3 inches of soil. Water and cover with a plastic bag till you see the first green leaves. Transplant to a 10- or 12-inch-wide pot, keep it warm and watered, and you'll have a beautiful indoor ginger plant that will produce "hands" you can harvest and use in cooking.

Moses helps plant a ginger "hand."

FOOLPROOF HERBS

Herbs, when watered faithfully (but never left standing in water), are an almost foolproof plant for your grandchild to grow indoors. Rosemary, thyme, sage, oregano, anise hyssop, lemon verbena, basil, mint, marjoram, monarda, lavender, pineapple sage, bay, and a host of edible, scented pelargoniums will root readily and adapt to an indoor lifestyle.

Slide out that crisper drawer in your fridge and give some of your herbs a second chance at life. Remove the herbs and spread them on a plate. Pick through them and choose which ones to plant. Feel the herbs and make sure they are supple and still have life within; you don't want to set your youngster up for failure.

Fill clean pots, cans, or jugs (making sure you have drainage holes) with potting soil and have your child water them until the soil is drenched. Use your pencil dibber to poke a hole about 2 inches deep in the center of the potting mix. Make a clean cut at the base of each herb stem and let your helper pick off the bottom leaves or needles, stand the herb in the hole, backfill with soil, and tamp it down gently.

Water once more, and set the herb pots on a gravel-filled tray in a brightly lit southern or western exposure (away from the direct blast of a heater or air conditioner).

Remember to do the finger poke test to see if your plants need moisture, and water only when the top inch of the soil is dry. Have your helper turn the pots once a week so cuttings don't lean in one direction. (This is a great way to illustrate and talk about heliotropism, the phenomenon of plants turning toward the sun.) When your herbs are growing strongly, transplant them to a pot just slightly larger than the current one. (Small plants in large pots are doomed because the soil stays soggy and drowns the plant roots.) Feed with a weak solution of fish emulsion and kelp (keep fertilizer off leaves).

Once your herbs are established, make a tradition of having mini harvests from your plants for cooking or for drying and preserving. Show your child how to use a pair of small scissors to trim off leaves and flowers, and spread them to dry on newspaper or a screen in a warm, dark area. Take time daily to check on the drying herbs together. When the leaves or needles feel papery, they're finished and ready to be stored in a lidded tin or a glass container away from sunlight and heat. Have your grandchild make a handmade label for the jar and put his "Grown by _____" on it.

Scented pelargonium, dianthus, and rose petals dry on a screen. After drying, the petals will be used for salad toppings, decorating cakes, and pudding.

"The hands-on experience of gardening and
cooking teaches children the value and
pleasure of good food almost effortlessly."

ALICE WATERS
The Art of Simple Food

KIDS IN THE GARDEN

My grandmother's garden was a source of wonder and joy. Nearly every day, we explored the yard together and picked whatever was ripe and ready to be preserved or eaten fresh. Like most kids, I wasn't particularly thrilled about tasting something as strange-looking as a "Brown Turkey" fig or an alligator-skinned avocado. But, because they grew in Grandmother's garden and because she tasted them gleefully and offered me a bite, well, I couldn't resist.

Her garden was a good size, but separated into small beds that skirted fruit trees and long, narrow beds that flanked pathways and hugged walls. Pots, huddled companionably together near the porch and patio, provided an endless trial area for growing vegetables, flowers, and herbs. It was in the small beds and container areas that I learned the basics of plant care—call it Tending 101.

I wanted my grandchildren to think of my garden as magical too—full of opportunities, tastes, sights, and scents that would lodge themselves in their hearts. I didn't want a garden to mean work. I wanted a garden to be synonymous with joy.

Most of us probably don't have the time or space my grandmother had so many years ago. To make gardening simpler for modern, time-challenged grandmothers, I suggest using half barrels and other large containers. They are small spaces to weed, watch, and water, and provide an up-close-and-personal gardening experience. I love the daily intimate connection a child can have with a half barrel, bushel basket, hay bale, or container of plants. No pest, bloom, fruit, or flower will escape notice, especially if that child has an interested grown-up to share the experience.

Take time together and plant a Snack Pot of carrots, radishes, and snow peas to feast on all summer long. Reach deep into the soil of your Tater Tots tub and tug out some of the fresh little potatoes for cooking. "Cut-and-come again" greens sound like what they are—harvest your salad fixings and they'll regrow again and again. Grow and bake some mini pumpkins in-the-shell or spaghetti squash for an Italian Restaurant Night. Experiment with new spices and herbs, and taste, taste, taste. More than great food comes out of a healthy garden and a life-filled kitchen. As poet Amber Coverdale Sumrall wrote, "You know the most delectable miracles that take place in the kitchen are born when the heart is well fed."

Harvesting herbs, lettuce, and edible flowers is almost as much fun as eating them.

PREPARING YOUR POTS
A Short Course

These general directions should be followed when planting any of the vegetables in this chapter. So mark this page and return here often.

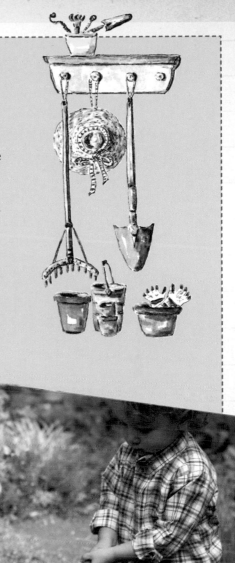

- Choose a few half barrels or large pots for a mini garden for your grandchild.

- Situate your pots in an area that receives at least 6 hours of sun a day and that is visible and accessible to your grandchild (such as a play area, patio, or area close to the kitchen).

- Make sure all pots have drainage holes.

- Cover drainage holes with a piece of screen or an old nylon.

- Add a few inches of gravel to the bottom of the pot.

- Fill your pot to the rim with bagged potting soil (available in garden and home centers and nurseries).

- Let your grandchild water until the soil is thoroughly drenched.

Watering is every child's favorite chore.

QUICK-STOP SNACK POTS

I t's time to let the special child in your life know that the best snacks don't come from a carton or bag, but straight from the earth. I've found that the veggies my grandchildren will not eat from a plate are a treasured commodity outdoors in the garden. The raised containers bring the yummy foods right up to a tot's height, impossible to ignore. They can swoop past a pot, stop, survey what is available, and pluck a snack that is fresh, tasty, and shhhh, don't tell them, *healthy*.

I always choose plants for Snack Pots that are easy to grow (a must for children) and have high nutritional benefits like proteins, amino acids, fiber, antioxidants, and vitamins—sort of a counterbalance to the foods youngsters often like to consume.

Once your child becomes used to the idea of fresh-snacking, he may start to consider many other options for the containers.

🌿 PLANT IT!
You will need three large pots, wooden boxes, or half barrels with drainage holes to hold the goodies in the snack garden.

Everything tastes better fresh from the garden—even things kids don't normally eat.

Pot 1

SNOW PEAS AND STRAWBERRIES

Top billing in your snacking garden goes to your crop of lofty and delicious snow peas, which need a sturdy trellis to climb.

Choose a big container and locate it in full sun. Place your trellis at the back of the pot. Snow peas thrive in cool weather and can be planted in early spring. Sow the seeds 1 inch deep and 3 to 4 inches apart at the base of the trellis, and mulch lightly. Water with a sprinkler or fine spray from your hose nozzle to avoid dislodging the seeds.

When the snow peas are up and climbing, explain to your helpers that their crop will do best when watered regularly. And, the more they pick and eat, the more the peas will grow. So encourage them to snack on the tasty pods whenever they're outside playing. The tender young shoots, tendrils, and leaves are yummy too.

To prolong your harvest, plant more snow peas every two weeks until summer becomes hot and the peas begin to wither. Sow more seeds in late summer for a tasty autumn crop.

Strawberry Skirts

Skirt your pot of snow peas with some mouthwateringly delicious strawberries, which are always a favorite of children. Strawberries flourish in the loose, rich soil of a container, but you will need to keep the soil evenly moist for them to do their best.

Get a head start on the harvest by buying strawberry plants in 4- to 6-inch pots. Choose a mixture of June-bearing and everbearing plants, which will produce throughout the summer. Tuck them along the border of the container about 6 inches apart. Water gently.

Once your berries start producing, pick, pick, pick, and fertilize them twice a month.

Faerie Berries

Tiny alpine strawberries, or as my grandchildren refer to them, "faerie berries," will thrive in even a small bucket filled with good soil and produce thimble-sized berries for months. Try 'Alexandria,' 'Baron Solemacher,' or 'Semperflorens,' or whichever varieties are available locally. You can start these from seed or 4-inch plants. Split the clumps of berries and set them into the soil at crown height.

A circle of faerie berries grows on a moss-covered wire frame.

Pot 2

TOMATO BLISS

I couldn't stand store-bought tomatoes when I was a child, but when I ran through the pathways of Grandmother's garden, I always gorged on her cherry tomatoes. The taste of the sweet, sun-warmed fruit is deeply entwined in my garden memories. What would summer be without tomatoes?

Try some of the tiny, indeterminate (they produce throughout the growing season) tomatoes, such as 'Tomatoberry' (strawberry shaped), 'Red Grape,' 'Yellow Pear,' 'Sun Gold,' and pastel 'Jolly Pink.' They produce for months on end, till the first frosts of autumn stop them cold. Just keep picking. Choose young plants that look robust, are bright green, and have a stocky, compact shape (not leggy).

🌿 PLANT IT!

In the world of tomatoes, a half barrel would be perfect for a threesome of the hearty plants. (See Prepare Your Pots, page 141.) You'll need lots and lots of sun for a healthy and prolific snacking tomato. Don't plant your young tomatoes outdoors until days are warm and soil temperatures are 75 to 80 degrees. Let your child dig holes two times wider and deeper than the root ball of the tomato seedlings you will be transplanting.

Have your grandchild spread his index and middle fingers, allowing the tomato's stem and leaves to poke down through them. Gently turn the seedlings upside down and tap the bottom of the pot to loosen soil. Slowly slide the plant out of the pot. The spread fingers will keep the tomato from falling.

Set the plant into the hole, and cover the stem of the tomato until only the top two pairs of leaves poke through the soil. Burying your plant deeply will encourage lots of healthy roots to grow from each of the buried nodes. Your young plant will grow strong and tall and will be able to withstand winds and the heavy load it will bear when it starts producing. You may wish to plant only one tomato plant in your snacking pot, but if you're adding others, allow at least 12 inches between them.

BUMBLEBEE RUMBA

As soon as your tomatoes begin to bloom, you will be visited by busy, fuzzy-rumped bumblebees. Sit with your child and notice how the bumbles grab each yellow blossom and dance wildly. The bumble will get dusted with golden pollen and carry the cargo to other blooms, thus ensuring lots of yummy tomatoes.

Okay, so that big, green caterpillar with the scary, but harmless, horn is eating the leaves of your tomato plant. You're the lucky host to a future sphinx moth, one of the best pollinators in a garden. If you have enough, donate a tomato plant to this hungry critter. Cover the plant with cheesecloth or screen and let him have at it. After the caterpillar disappears, take off the screen. Someday you'll be rewarded with the quiet, graceful presence of a long-tongued visitor who more closely resembles a hummingbird than an insect.

Tomatoes need a sturdy support. I like to use stout branches or bamboo stakes, but you can buy a tomato cage from a garden center. Tomatoes are also hearty feeders, so you'll need to douse them with a liquid fish emulsion and kelp fertilizer twice a month. I always mulch around my container-grown tomatoes to keep them moist and free of weeds. One good way to get your grandchild to water the plants deeply is to ask him to count to twenty slowly as he floods the containers. Show your child how to pinch (not cut or pull) the small suckers that form in the V of a tomato's short side branches. These little guys are all show and no go. They'll never produce fruit, but they will use a lot of the tomato's energy to produce foliage. Pinch them out! Also pinch off the growing tips of the tomato branches if they become unruly.

A rustic trellis, made with driftwood, supports a heavy crop of cherry tomatoes.

Pot 3

BURIED TREASURES: RADISHES AND CARROTS

Sweet carrots and radishes straight from the soil, washed with cool, clear water, and popped into a little mouth—what could be better? When I planted my first children's Teaching Garden at my community gardens in Cambria, California, I included big pots of radishes and carrots. I kept seeding them successively so that the 4-H girls and classes of grammar school kids could have them available for snacking any time they craved them, which was often.

With my grandchildren, I don't plant the usual radishes and carrots commonly found in a grocery store, but special ones of many shapes and colors—pastel radishes, radishes that when sliced look just like a piece of ripe watermelon, and two-toned carrots in purple and orange. I want snack treats that nurture a child's soul as well as body.

🌿 PLANT IT!

To prepare your pot, see page 141.

Give your child a kitchen fork that is slightly bent at the tip and show him how to "rake" the soil in the pot lightly, making mini fork-sized furrows, which are the perfect depth for both carrot and radish seeds.

Always check the information on the back of seed packets, which will give you planting guidelines and tell you how long it takes your snack crops to mature. But you don't have to wait (and most kids won't) to harvest. Even the tiniest baby carrots and radishes can be tugged out and nibbled. (Just remember to always wash produce.)

"For optimum health, scientists say, eat a rainbow of colors. Your plate should look like a box of Crayolas." —Janice Horowitz

Rake little furrows for planting seeds with a bent kitchen fork.

To make planting tiny seeds easier for little hands, pour clean sand and seeds into a grated cheese container or spice jar with a shaker top. Fill another shaker-top jar with some of your dry, bagged potting soil. Now have your child shake the container of seeds and sand onto the soil. Use the second container to top the seeds with a thin layer of soil and let your child pat them gently into the ground. Water with a fine spray from a hose or a rose-head watering can. Do it gently so that the seeds are not unearthed.

You should have radishes sprouting within 5 days. They'll pop through the crust of soil and make breaking into the light a little easier for the carrots, which take a longer time to germinate. As your child picks from the pots, sow more seeds to keep the snacks coming.

Radishes don't like hot weather, and when it hits, they become bitter and hot. Retire the radishes' planting spot in the pot, top it with new soil, and replant them at the end of summer.

Little Nibbles

When it comes to carrots, children inevitably love the minis—perhaps it is the almost faerie-like aspect of something they usually see in a much larger size. Plant the seeds of 'Little Fingers,' which have a sweet flavor and reach only 3 to 4 inches, or 'Cosmic Purple,' which, you guessed it, have a deep purple skin paired with a rich orange interior and a spicy-sweet taste. 'Minicor' is tasty from the time it is the size of a matchstick till it reaches the girth of a five-year-old's fingers.

TATER TOTS

You can use your finger to test your soil's moisture (see page 136), or you can tech it up a bit and buy an inexpensive moisture meter from a garden center. The benefit of the meter is that its metal probe dips deep into your pot's soil and lets you monitor what is going on far down in the root zone.

'Cranberry Red,' 'Easter Egg,' 'Yukon Gold,' 'Rose Finn,' 'Swedish Peanut,' 'Blue'—the world of potatoes isn't just brown and boring; it is a rainbow of color and a symphony of tastes. You can find an amazing array of potato varieties in online catalogs and garden centers. Once your child harvests a homegrown basket of spuds, you will all experience a sampling of Potato Heaven.

If you are visiting a grocery store and find some great potatoes you want to grow, go ahead and buy them. Many store-bought potatoes are treated with a growth inhibitor to keep them from sprouting. Scrub the potatoes gently with a soft brush, dry them, and cut out about a 1½-inch piece that sports at least two "eyes" (growth buds). Set the pieces into separate sections of an egg carton (they can be sprouted with or without soil), and ask your grandchild to check on the potatoes daily to see if the eyes have sprouted.

Egg cartons make perfect sprouting cradles.

🌿 PLANT IT!

Half barrels are perfect containers for a good-sized crop of potatoes. Fill your pot about a quarter full of bagged soil mixed with aged, bagged manure. Place the pot in an area that gets six hours of sunlight, preferably a morning sun site. Set your sprouted potatoes "eyes to the sky" or seed potatoes about 6 inches apart on top of the soil, and cover them with a scant inch of soil, which will make them emerge quickly. Water gently when planted, and check daily to make sure the soil is moist, but not sopping wet.

Don't worry about your soil level being too low; you will continue to add layers of soil to the pot each time the potato vines grow 5 to 6 inches. Mound the soil and some manure over the potatoes, leaving about 2 inches of the vine uncovered each time. Within a few weeks, the first star-shaped blooms will appear, and soon your crop of potatoes will begin to fatten below the soil.

If you and your grandchild are curious about what is happening underground, just stick your hands into the soil and feel for the tiny tubers, your own buried treasure. You can pull out a few and cook them, but you won't do your real harvest till the potato vine withers and dies in the fall.

When it is time to harvest, you can reach in and pull out potatoes, or use a garden fork to lift them out. Dry the potatoes on a tarp or newspaper in a dark, dry area (never let eating potatoes sit in the light, or toxins will form). Store the potatoes in a dark, cool closet, cellar, or container, but NEVER in the refrigerator.

Potato Volcanoes

I haven't met many children who aren't crazy about mashed, or as my son used to say, "smashed," potatoes, but just in case your child is the exception, once he grows and cooks his own, he will be a potato missionary.

I always work with my grandchild as a potato mashing team. I prefer to use a wire masher, rather than electric beaters, to keep the potatoes cloud-soft and never gluey. Using yogurt in the potatoes makes them creamy, delectable, and almost effortless.

Makes volcanoes for 4.

INGREDIENTS

1½ pounds potatoes (Yukon Golds make super mashers)

2 tablespoons unsalted butter

2 tablespoons half-and-half or milk

2 tablespoons plain low-fat yogurt

Salt and pepper to taste

1 to 1½ cups good melting cheese (Muenster, Cheddar, Monterey Jack)

Ketchup in a squeeze bottle

Preheat oven to 350°F.

Show your child how to clean potatoes with a small scrub brush. Granny should be the one to cut the potatoes into chunks of the same size so they will cook evenly.

Fill a large pot with enough water to cover the potatoes and bring to a boil. Cook potatoes about 15 to 20 minutes until fork tender.

Heat the butter and milk till warm.

Remove the cooked potatoes from the stove and drain over a colander in the sink. Pour the drained potatoes back into the original cooking pot.

Mix the warmed milk and butter into the yogurt and slowly pour the mixture into the potatoes as your child mashes. Let him use an ice cream scoop to mound the potatoes into small volcanoes on a lightly oiled cookie sheet. Use a spoon to make holes in the top (the craters).

Sprinkle the crater and sides of the volcanoes with grated cheese. Slip the cookie sheet into the preheated oven for a few minutes until the cheese melts. Quickly squirt thin threads of ketchup (lava) into the crater and down the side of the volcano. Eat them while they're hot.

Scoop three different sized balls of mashed potato to form the snowman's body. Use fruits, a tiny carrot, and red bell pepper for features, celery for arms, and a cracker for a hat.

PUMPKIN PATCH IN A POT

Don't let anyone tell you that you can't grow pumpkins in pots. I've grown the 'Rouge Vif d'Etampes' (aka 'Cinderella's Carriage') in a big half barrel filled with rich soil. I also have had great success with mini pumpkins in large terra-cotta pots, half barrels, and a trash can. My best pumpkin ever, a queen-sized beauty, grew in our compost bin (okay, that was an accident, but a fabulous one).

In late spring, many garden centers offer a variety of young pumpkin plants in 4- to 6-inch pots. As soon as your soil warms and all danger of frost is past, you can plant these outdoors in containers appropriate to the mature size of the pumpkins. Big pumpkin = big pot.

🌿 PLANT IT!

Choose half barrels or big pots for your large pumpkins. Limit yourself to only one of the large variety of pumpkins per pot. Smaller varieties of pumpkins will thrive in containers at least 12 to 14 inches across. I sometimes grow the tiny ones in an old wheelbarrow or child's wagon.

Late spring or early summer is the time to plant seeds. Most varieties take between 80 and 120 days to mature. Plant each seed in a yogurt cup or small pot (with drainage holes, of course) filled with bagged potting soil. Water the seeds and set them outdoors in a sunny spot. Keep the soil moist, but not soggy. When the vines have at least two sets of true leaves (the first leaves to pop up are smooth and oval, and the second set of leaves are true leaves), you can plant them into their containers, which must be in full sun.

Fill the container as described on page 141, but make a mound of soil in the center of the pot. Gently water the mound of soil, and tuck in two plants per mound. Pat the soil around the pumpkins and water again thoroughly. Fertilize monthly with fish emulsion and kelp. If you are planting miniature pumpkins, place a sturdy trellis in the back of the container. The plants will clamber up and over a trellis, and the pumpkins will dangle from the vines like a collection of holiday ornaments.

As long as the pumpkins have plenty of food, water (they are always thirsty), and sunshine, they will thrive. Water at the base of the vine or use a soaker hose, but try not to do any overhead watering or fungus and mildew may develop.

In late July, go out to the pumpkin patch and have your child scratch his name into the tender skin of the green globes (if he's too young to write, you should scratch his name, as well as the names of his siblings and other grandchildren—one name per globe). As the pumpkins swell, the names will grow, and at the beginning of October, the brilliant red-orange superstars of the garden can be claimed by their proud namesake owners.

In autumn, test the pumpkins for ripeness. Knock on one and listen for the hollow *thunk* that signals that it's ready to be picked. Push against the skin; it should feel taut and hard. Use clippers to harvest pumpkins, and be sure to leave a few inches of the vine attached, which will help keep them from rotting. If you want your pumpkins to last, cure them in a cool, dry area for 2 to 3 weeks.

After the pumpkins are "engraved" with your grandchild's name, the writing will harden and rise like a tough scar.

Pumpkin Crunchies

Every pleasure is magnified when kids are allowed to enjoy themselves with their friends. This goes especially for pumpkin carving. A great way to reward the industrious carvers is with these pumpkin seed treats.

Crunchy toasted pumpkin seeds burst with flavor and nutrients, and they are high in vitamins, minerals, protein, and fiber. They have a sweetish, nutty taste, and add great texture and crunch to every dish. (I add them as a topping to soups, salads, casseroles, rice and quinoa dishes, and even breakfast cereal.) They're at their best fresh from the oven dusted lightly with salt.

INGREDIENTS

Fresh pumpkin seeds

Olive or canola oil (spray cans make this easier for kids)

Sea or kosher salt (light dusting)

Help your youngster cut the top off a ripe pumpkin and use an ice-cream scoop to remove the seeds. Put the seeds, which will be gooey and sometimes stringy, into a colander. Run water over them and let your grandchild moosh them around till they're free of strings and flesh.

Spread the seeds on a parchment-paper-lined cookie sheet and let them sit until dry. Once they're dry, spray them lightly with olive oil and sprinkle them with salt. Slide the cookie sheet into the oven set at 200°F. After half an hour, use a spatula to move the seeds around, and roast them for another half hour until golden, but not dark (they get bitter if they burn).

Remove the seeds from the oven and let them cool. Store in a jar in the refrigerator.

Faerie Carriages

If you grow tiny pumpkins like 'Munchkin' or the white 'Baby Boo,' you and your grandchild can quickly bake them for individual desserts for your family and friends. The flesh of these charming little self-contained dishes is delicious when enhanced with the tang of oranges and the sweetness of maple syrup tinged with vanilla.

INGREDIENTS FOR 1 PUMPKIN

One mini-pumpkin per person (with stem)

Pinch of grated nutmeg (I recommend that you grate whole nutmeg seeds. Children love this task.)

Pinch of ground cinnamon

Sea salt

2 teaspoons fresh orange juice and a pinch of zest

¼ teaspoon vanilla (pure vanilla extract imparts the best flavor)

⅛ teaspoon maple syrup

Dab of unsalted butter

Fresh whipped cream or ice cream

On the day of your gathering, cut the pumpkin stems to about 1 inch. Gently slice off the top of your minis (about half of the way down) and let your grandchild scoop out the seeds and any strings.

Preheat oven to 350°F. Place the pumpkins on a parchment- or foil-covered cookie sheet. Let your helper sprinkle nutmeg, cinnamon, and sea salt into each pumpkin. Spoon in orange juice, vanilla, and a pinch of orange zest. Drizzle maple syrup inside each one and put a dab of butter on top. Put a square of parchment or foil atop each pumpkin (otherwise the top might fall inside), then replace the cut top.

Bake about 40 to 50 minutes. Remove from the oven, lift the tops, and let them rest for about 10 minutes. Fill each pumpkin with whipped cream or ice cream and a light drizzle of maple syrup. Yum!

LARGE, SMALL, SHORT AND TALL

Grow a big 'Rouge Vif d'Etampes' in a large pot, or try a shining white 'Lumina,' which will grow to 12 pounds. 'Baby Bear' reaches 2½ pounds, and 'Long Island Cheese' at 7 pounds looks like a round of buff-colored cheese. 'Jarrahdale' is silvery-blue with a girth of 10 to 12 inches. 'Small Sugar Pie' is my favorite for baking. 'Jack Be Little,' 'Munchkin,' 'Little Boo,' and 'Baby Pam' are hand-sized and lovable.

A child's wagon makes a perfect planter for mini pumpkins.

CIAO (CHOW) BELLA!

I talian food. Just writing those two words makes my mouth water. When I was young and Nonie or Grandmother would promise me "any food I wanted for my birthday," I always chose Italian. Ummm, luscious sauce flecked with garlic, specks of oregano, and a sprinkling of freshly ground Parmesan cheese.

When you and your grandchild grow some of the ingredients for your Italian Restaurant Night menu (See "Kids in the Kitchen," page 97), you'll be amazed by the rich aroma, taste, and texture of your meal.

🌿 PREPARE YOUR POTS!

You'll need a couple of half barrels to grow your own ingredients for tasty Italian dinners. Give your youngster a feeling of immediate success by buying small, robust tomato plants from a garden center. Don't plant them outdoors until all danger of frost is past and nighttime temperatures are above 55°F. (See planting directions for tomatoes, on page 145.)

Spaghetti squash, oregano, basil, and plum tomatoes are snuggled companionably together in a huge pot filled with rich, bagged potting soil.

Pot 1

PLUM OR PASTE TOMATOES

Not all tomatoes are created equal. The small tomatoes described on page 144 are great for snacking but not for cooking. At the nursery, guide your grandchild to a Roma or paste tomato known to make great sauce. I usually choose the 'San Marzano,' 'Juliet,' 'Viva Italia,' 'Roma,' 'Giant Paste,' 'Italian Giant Red Pear,' or 'Amish Paste.' To open your child's eyes to the diverse array of tomatoes available (over 14,000 varieties), look in catalogs and online at the Seed Savers Exchange website, www.seedsavers.org. The site boasts over 70 varieties of weird and wonderful tomato choices in a kaleidoscope of colors. Buy some early producers like 'Beaverlodge Plum' (this is especially important if your grandchild is around only in the early summer), then add some later varieties. Catalogs and nursery labels will tell you whether you have an early or late-maturing variety.

Help your youngster plant the tomatoes deep into the soil and learn how to care for them (see page 146).

Pot 2

SPAGHETTI SQUASH

What will your grandchild say when you tell him that you're going to plant some homegrown spaghetti? Plant spaghetti? Spaghetti grows? Not all spaghetti grows, but the big yellow vegetable marrow called golden macaroni or spaghetti squash is a spaghetti that grows and grows and grows.

You'll need a big pot for this one big plant (if your pot is big enough, you can include other plants). Set the pot in full sun, and give the squash some room to roam. The vine will spill over the sides of the barrel and start to meander. If the vine starts to take over your yard, cut it back.

WHAT'S UP YOUR SLEEVE?

Make an aluminum foil sleeve and wrap it around your young tomato plants. Be sure to bury the foil at least 1 inch into the soil. The sleeve will protect tender young stems from destructive cutworms and tomato blight.

This trick was first introduced to me by my friend Jane Taylor, the founder of the Michigan State 4-H Children's Garden. You can show your youngster some of the magic that happens when a basil seed is planted in the soil and watered. Shake some basil seeds into your grandchild's hand. Add a few drops of water, making sure to cover the little specks of black, and wait. In less than a minute, the basil seeds will change into what look like tiny tadpoles still encased in their protective covering of goo. Now you can plant them!

Fino verde basil has small leaves and a big punch of flavor.

Don't try to rush Mother Nature. Your squash won't be happy if it's planted during cold weather. Wait until the days warm and the nights stay above 50°F. Fill the container with bagged potting soil. Scoop extra soil into a mound in the center of the pot. Help your child nestle one or two spaghetti squash seedlings into the mound and water thoroughly. If you're planting seeds, tuck two or three seeds into the mound about 1 inch deep. Try the variety called 'Orangetti' for brilliant flesh high in carotene, or 'Stripetti,' a spaghetti squash that will keep for months. Water as needed.

Squash are greedy feeders and will need a dose of natural fertilizer monthly. Your squash should turn from a buff color to a bright golden yellow when it is ripe (this takes about 88 days), and the skin will be too tough to pierce with a fingernail. (See page 99 for how to prepare and serve this spaghetti squash.)

Pot 3

A MINI ITALIAN HERB GARDEN

Tomato sauce is tomato sauce. But tomato sauce with a sprinkling of homegrown herbs, like basil, oregano, and garlic, will open up a new world of tastes.

If you slowly ease your child into the habit of going outdoors to pick fresh herbs to add to meals, which is a chore they'll love, you'll give a gift of taste that will span a lifetime of eating.

Basil

When your nights warm to about 50°F, visit your local garden center and buy some small pots of basil plants (see Preparing Your Pots, page 141). You can grow all kinds of flavors of basil, from cinnamon and lemon to clove and licorice, but for cooking Italian sauces, the old favorite, sweet basil, still tops the list.

Space the plants about 6 to 8 inches apart. Settle them into the soil at the same height as the pot they came in. Basil thrives and becomes bushy and compact when it is regularly trimmed for cooking and fed monthly with a high-nitrogen, natural plant food.

Add basil leaves not only to your spaghetti sauces, but also to salads, summer plates of tomatoes drizzled with olive oil and vinegar, and sandwiches, salsas, and your own homemade vinegar.

Garlic

Take your grandchild for a visit to your local farmers market or grocery store and choose some plump, firm heads of organic garlic to plant. Before planting, let your youngster separate the cloves, but leave the papery peel intact. Use a pencil to poke holes in the soil about 2 inches deep for each clove. Show your grandchild the top and bottom of the clove (top is pointed, bottom is blunt) and have her place the cloves with the bottom down, and then cover them with soil. You can plant garlic throughout the container because its knitting-needle green leaves are not pushy and it will thrive snuggled in a pot among your other herbs.

Don't worry about harvesting your garlic bulbs, which take months to mature. Instead, make a habit of clipping the tender green tops for cooking. You can also use the tiny green bulbs, but you'll need to replant cloves as you use the bulbs. The green garlic is a subtle and tasty addition to sauces when added in the last few minutes of cooking.

Oregano

Visit the herb trays at your local garden center and show your youngster how to release the scent of oregano by rubbing the leaves. It might smell familiar since it's the taste of a good pizza sauce.

Your oregano will be happy planted near the edge of your container. Oregano thrives when cut regularly and watered only as needed.

GREAT EXPECTATIONS

During the times of the Egyptian pharoahs, laborers and slaves building the pyramids were fed garlic, which they believed would increase their stamina and protect them from disease. Romans included garlic as one of the most important foods of a soldier's or laborer's diet. In Europe, superstitious runners chew on cloves of garlic with the belief that nobody will be able to pass them. In Hungary, horse jockeys believe that if they pin a clove of garlic to their clothes or the horse's bit, they will outrun their competition.

BARRELS, BUCKETS, AND BALES
Salad Gardens for All Seasons

For many years, it was difficult to buy any but the most common lettuces and greens, but that has all changed. Now a world of possibilities exists when planning and planting a small, child-friendly salad garden in your own backyard. A container salad garden is one of the quickest, easiest, first, and last of the year to produce delicious ingredients for your meals.

A GREEN BY ANY OTHER NAME . . .

You can call the tiny rosettes of green mâche a name like corn salad or a child's favorite name, lamb's lettuce. But whatever you call it, be sure to include it in your planter or bale. Mâche is the most tender, succulent green, and so tolerant of cold that my friend Suzanne tells me that in Switzerland she could reach into a snow bank and pull out a plant for supper. Lamb's lettuce self-sows readily. You'll have more volunteers next growing season.

🌿 PLANT IT!

Half barrels or big pots will work well for salad greens, but remember a wide surface area is a must for your garden to fill out. (See Preparing Your Pots, page 141.)

Make a spring visit to your local garden center with your youngster and cruise through the seed racks and the vegetable section to find lettuces, herbs, edible flowers, and greens of interest. I'll have to admit that the choices are often made because of names. What child could resist a lettuce called Deer Tongue, Red Giant, Sweet Valentine, 'Little Gem,' or Firecracker, or kale and chard with names like Lark's Tongue, Ragged Jack, Pot of Gold, and Scarlet Charlotte? Tuck in seeds or plants of edible flowers and herbs such as borage, dill, calendula, Johnny-jump-up, dianthus, and nasturtium to jazz up your salads' colors and tastes. (See greens and edible flowers on pages 163.)

Instead of needing full sun like most vegetables, lettuce and greens will thrive in the dappled shade of a tree or under a tepee of vines. Place your salad garden close to a water source. The surest way to ruin a crop of greens, or make them bitter, is to overheat them or deprive them of water. The soil should be moist but not soggy, keep your child's watering can filled, sitting nearby, and ready for action.

WATERCRESS GARDEN

Find an old pot or tub that will hold water. Plant watercress—the peppery flavored old-fashioned green that is perfect in salads—in heavy, wet soil mixed with sand. Set the pot in a shady area and keep the soil soggy (set under a dripping faucet). Within weeks, you and your child will have your first harvest of cress. Here's a fun kid recipe to do with your cress.

Watercress Nests. Hard-boil six eggs, cool, and have the kids peel the shells. Cut eggs in half lengthwise. Show kids how to pop out the yolks and push them through a sieve, add a dollop of mayonnaise, and mash with a fork till the yolks hold together. Mold into tiny "eggs." Place the molded eggs inside the halved whites and nestle curly cress around the eggs. Dress lightly and include these nests in one of your picnics.

Buckets, half barrels, and pots of greens nestle outside the kitchen door.

Give your greens and herbs room to show their stuff. Help your grandchild plant them at least 8 inches apart, and set the tallest plants at the back of the container. After tucking the plants into their holes, backfill any open space around the root-ball with bagged potting soil or compost. Water your plants into their new homes. Go outside with your youngster daily to make sure the newcomers are moist.

GREENS AND EDIBLE FLOWERS

With these fabulous greens, you'll be able to host a Salad Bar Party (see "Kids in the Kitchen," page 101) and share them with your friends and family.

Always rinse greens after cutting them. Let your grandchild cull any damaged or wilted leaves and then spin them dry. Tuck them into a pillowcase or dish towel, gently roll it closed, and put in the refrigerator's crisper drawer. Use as soon as possible.

If you are sowing seeds rather than planting pots of salad greens, simply follow the directions on the back of the seed packet, which will tell you when and how deep to plant the seeds. Sift some bagged potting soil in a light layer over the seeds. Water them gently.

Within just a couple of weeks after planting nursery stock or about a month after planting from seed, you'll be able to start some cut-and-come-again harvesting. Trim about one-third of the lettuce leaves off gently with blunt, child-friendly scissors. Your salad fixings will regrow and can be harvested a couple more times before the plants need replacing.

When seedlings first appear, you'll need to thin them if they're too crowded in your container. (They should be at least 2 to 3 inches apart.) A young gardener sometimes feels like a plant parent, and thinning plants can be traumatic. Explain that plants need room to grow successfully. The easiest way to remove extra plants from the garden without disturbing the roots of other plants is to use small scissors or clippers to snip them.

Viola, dianthus, bachelor's button, chive blooms, and nasturtiums add color and taste to any salad.

SALAD GARDEN

SALAD GARDEN

Spring greens

'Black Seeded Simpson'
'Buttercrunch'
chard
endive
escarole
'Green Oak Leaf'
'Lollo Rosso'
mâche
mesclun mix
'Red Oak Leaf'
spinach

Summer greens

arugula
buttercrunch
curly cress
'Marvel of Four Seasons'
miner's lettuce
radicchio
'Red Sails'
romaine
'Rouge d'Hiver'

Fall and winter greens

Belgian endive
curly endive
escarole
mâche
Treviso chicory
'Winter Density'

BALE PLANTING

"**W**hat's old is new again" is an apt adage for dedicated gardener Rose Marie McGee's bountiful kitchen garden, a rainbow of lettuces and greens planted in wheat straw bales. Imagine a container that will not only nourish crop after crop of healthy plants, but also break down and nourish the soil of your garden.

Take your grandchild (and a truck or station wagon) to a local feed store, farm supply store, or farm stand and buy a bale (or two or ten) of wheat straw. I like wheat versus hay and alfalfa because it doesn't harbor lots of weeds.

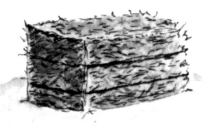

Decide where you want to put your bale garden (remember greens will do fine in dappled shade). Lay your bale on its long side and keep the baling wire or twine intact; don't cut it off or your bale will collapse. (This is the only instance when I go for synthetic binding, which will last through many seasons.)

Scratch deeply into the upper (planting) surface of the bale with a garden fork to break it apart so that water can soak in. Set a sprinkler near or on top of the bale and water it until it is soaked, but don't even think about planting. Your wet bale will heat up (part of the process of decomposition) and would injure fragile young roots. Water again in a few days and soak it thoroughly. Let your bale sit for another week and moisten it daily.

If you see a few little shoots of green wheat sprouting after the watering, just tug them out and throw them onto the compost pile.

After your week of waiting, let your youngster use a child-sized garden fork to scratch into the planting surface of the bale. (Although you already did this chore, your child needs to feel like a part of this process.)

Dig some planting holes, fill the holes with bagged potting soil, and water the entire top of the bale deeply. (If you're putting in seeds, don't dig planting holes. Just add a 3- to 4-inch layer of bagged soil to the top of the bale and let your helper water it thoroughly.)

Plant your bale with a medley of edible flowers and herbs such as borage, nasturtium, chives, chervil, cilantro, and dill. Your plants will thrive throughout the summer and into the fall. Interplant with your favorite selection of lettuces and greens, which are at their best in cool weather from mid-spring to early summer and again in the fall. Sow successive crops of lettuce two weeks apart to lengthen their harvest season.

Check moisture level (see page 149) and water your plants as needed, but never let the bale dry out completely. Run a simple drip line around the planting area or keep it watered with a sprinkler, and, of course, let your child water the plants as needed.

THE GREAT MIGRATION

Many of the herbs you and your youngster have been growing outdoors can be lifted and transplanted into smaller pots indoors during the winter. Just plant them in bagged potting soil in a container with drainage, and set them in a sunny southern or western exposure. Continue to harvest tasty herbs for your meals throughout the winter.

"It took me four years to paint like Raphael,
but a lifetime to paint like a child."

PABLO PICASSO

CHAPTER SIX

RAINY DAY ACTIVITIES

at both of my grandmothers' homes, the kitchen table was always the center of activity. Whether we were cooking together, making pottery, drawing and painting, playing games, or cutting out paper and flower dolls, everything seemed to occur on that island of wood.

Things are no different at my home now. Outdoors, the huge, old farm table sits under an arbor just waiting for the welcome (and noisy) arrival of children. Indoors, on rainy days and starry nights, we have the long kitchen worktable where we play games, sculpt with pipe cleaners, model clay, and do art and cooking projects.

When my grandchildren were younger, I kept a mini "studio" for them in my tiny sunroom work area. They had a small table and chairs, just their size, a basket of brushes, clay, colored pencils, pens, watercolors, and lots of paper. When their legs got too long to fit under their table, they graduated to our kitchen table and continued the tradition started by my own grandmothers so many years ago. Even though they love working at the big people's table, they still reminisce about "the good old days in their studio."

GRANNY'S MAGICAL CRAFT BOX

Set up an area for your youngsters, or use your kitchen table, but make sure you're okay with the likelihood of a big mess and possible accidents. You can purchase huge rolls of kraft paper, also called butcher paper, from art stores to cover your floor, table, and whatever else you're worried about. Durable aprons will help minimize disasters, and you can decorate them for each child with fabric or acrylic paints.

Think outside the house too, and devote an outdoor space for the fresh-air art projects that kids so love to do. Your grandchild can stockpile stones, shells, twigs, rocks, leaves, seedpods, and whatever is beautiful, odd, and available to keep for future projects.

Set up a chalkboard area either on a wall or on the ground, and keep it filled with colorful sidewalk chalks or the exciting new 3-D chalks. A Chalk Cloth (see page 130) is the perfect indoor solution to creative or active indoor play.

Remember, whether indoors or out, step back and let your youngsters express themselves. No rules exist as to what is "good art" or bad. What is important is the doing and the sharing of time together. Stick people rather than anatomically correct drawings, lumps of clay that look like slugs instead of turtles—all these less-than-perfect creations fuel your child's imagination and instill a wonderful sense of confidence and achievement.

Children lose themselves, or find themselves, when they're totally immersed in creating.

Keep your indoor supplies nearby in open containers or boxes, which you can paint or decorate with collages cut from magazines or with original artwork. Outfit your containers with the list below.

SUPPLIES TO INSPIRE YOUR LITTLE GENIUSES:

- Camera for puppet- and bookmaking
- Chalks, regular and large colored sidewalk
- Chenille stems (pipe cleaners) in colors, with glittery finishes, from fat and huge to small and spindly
- Clay
- Cork board, aka Life Board (see page 4)
- Fasteners, round-head for making books
- Felt pieces of different colors and a felt board
- Glue, white, or glue sticks (glue sticks are wonderful, easy to use, and forgiving)
- Molded letters and cookie cutters that can be stamped onto clay
- Paint, acrylic (water soluble) for older children
- Paint, tempera for toddlers
- Paint, watercolors
- Paper, construction

- Paper, clear, contact, for preserving artwork or making "stained glass" windows
- Paper, drawing
- Paper, origami, of all colors and metallic finishes
- Paper punch, with round holes or stars, hearts, and other shapes
- Pencils, colored
- Pencils, Stubby Chubby for young artists
- Pencils, watercolor (apply like a pencil, but brush with water and work like watercolors)
- Pens, fabric marker (not washable)
- Pens, marker in gold, silver, and copper
- Pens, washable ink marker
- Ribbon, for tying books
- Rubber erasers
- Scissors, child-safe
- Tape
- Tape recorder for musical moments and story making

Chenille stems, colored pencils, paints, crayons, and an array of papers stand ready for young Picassos.

The Rule is NO RULES!

Tabling the Matter

This tablecloth project happened by accident, but it has turned into a family tradition. As I walked the aisles of our local paint store, I spied a stack of 4-by-12-foot canvas drop cloths. They were well made and very inexpensive. I bought one to cover our farm table so that when my grandchildren were doing their art projects we wouldn't worry about spills and spots.

What started out as a workhorse turned into a unicorn. The kids began using acrylics and markers to paint and draw on the cloth itself. The dropcloth turned into a beautiful tablecloth, an ongoing art project that will take many visits to complete, which will then provide a record of good times together.

YOU'LL NEED:

Large canvas dropcloth
Waterproof colored markers
Pens
Acrylic paints
Stiff brushes of varying sizes

Just let the kids dive in!

Family Portraits

Whether your grandchild comes once a week to visit or once a summer, growing kids change dramatically in a short time. That's why I love to photograph my grands and then ask them to do self-portraits to post alongside their photos on our art line (see below). After their portraits have been on display for a while, they are taken down and added to a keepsake portfolio of art, which I will someday pass on to them.

Give each grandchild a tablet of drawing paper and pencils, and arrange for short periods to create the portraits. No fair peeking while the drawing is going on, and no hints, rules, or critiques.

After the drawing is complete, pull out crayons, markers, or paints for the children to add touches of color. You'll be amazed by some of the insightful portraits your grandchild will make. Make sure your young artist always signs and dates each piece for posterity.

CHALK ONE UP FOR OUTDOOR ART

Find a sheltered area outdoors where you can cover a wall or a large piece of marine-grade plywood with chalkboard paint for your grandchild's murals or spot art. Outfit your outdoor art area with regular chalks, fat sidewalk chalks, a bucket of water, and sponges for erasing.

Art Lines

For children, it isn't just the creation that matters, but the fact that their work will be on display for everyone to admire. So, instead of taping their artwork to the wall or sticking it on the refrigerator, give it center stage billing on an art line.

To frame each art piece that will be displayed, simply glue it onto a colorful sheet of construction paper that is slightly larger than the work.

An ever-changing array of art hangs from the line.

YOU'LL NEED:

Two 2-inch screw hooks

Clothesline

Clothespins, wooden (let your kids paint or decorate the pins)

Screw in the hooks about 48 inches apart (most studs are 16 inches apart) at a child's eye height. Tie the clothesline to each hook and stretch it taut. Use the clothespins to hang your grandchild's latest artwork.

Twisted, Turned & Tied

O n rainy days, I sat for hours in my grandmother's breakfast nook and played with a boxful of plain white pipe cleaners. With a simple twist, splice, turn, or tie, I could make just about anything.

When I went to buy my grandchildren pipe cleaners, I found a new, zippier, longer, fatter, more colorful, and glittery version of the old standby. They're called chenille stems, fuzzy sticks, and the fat ones are Brain Noodles—they're all great. I bought two packets for each child, one brilliantly colored and one of the beglittered fancy stems. They've been used and reused until some of the stems are going bald.

Keep a big basket of these fuzzy sticks in your grandchild's play area. You'll be amazed at the multitude of creations she will design—jewelry, people, animals, crowns, glasses, wigs, watches, woven skirts, and more. So much magic can be created from something that a grown-up might overlook or dismiss as mundane. And speaking of grown-ups, why not pull out some chenille stems and create alongside your grandchildren— it's good to be a child with them sometimes.

Straight chenille stems will soon become crowns, epaulets, snakelike bracelets, and anklets.

Puppet Shows

Take full-body photographs of your grandchild, pets, friends, and family, and then enlarge them on a color copier so that they are paper doll size (about 4 inches). Help your grandchild glue the images to a stiff paper backing (like bristol board or cardboard) and cut them out. Glue the paper image onto a flat jumbo-sized "craft stick," or, for bigger images, use a paint stick. These stick puppets are perfect for rainy day puppet shows, which can be based on a beloved book or spontaneous, imaginary puppetry.

Drape a small table with a cloth on three sides to use as a stage. Leave the back open so your child can gain ready access to puppets. Line up chairs for the audience, and settle in for the show.

When a child puts on a costume, he becomes someone else and inhibitions vanish.

Acting Out Off Broadway

Cuddle up together with one of your favorite children's books (see page 4 for some choices). Read the book aloud in a dramatic way—abandon your dignity and change your voice and facial expressions to suit the characters. Coax your grandchild (if old enough to read) to do the same. For toddlers, just read a passage dramatically and encourage participation.

Use one of your storybooks as a basis for a rainy day off-Broadway production. Open up your Dress-up Drawers (see page 7), and let your grandchild enter into a fantasy land—with capes, oversized shirts, hats, and ribbons—whatever you have on hand.

Clear a "stage" space in your living room for the play. Roll up the rugs, move back the furniture, and focus a bright light on the "stage." Provide some appropriate music, and make some homemade theater signs with the title of the play and the name of the actors and actresses. Line up some chairs for the enthusiastic audience (YOU).

You'll be surprised by how readily even the shiest grandchild will act when given a chance and the complete attention of devoted fans. I was shocked when my timid three-year-old grandchild acted out some of the pages of Maurice Sendak's book *Where the Wild Things Are.* Another afternoon she followed through the pages of *Good Night, Gorilla* as though it was a script. My two oldest grandchildren donned clothes from the Dress-up Drawer, grabbed musical instruments from the Music Basket (see page 179), and performed improv from the top landing of the staircase.

Capes, wings, tiaras, and, of course, wands—are necessities for young faerie princesses.

I was amazed by their skill, ability to act, sing, and play instruments, and the joy they got from the show—and the attention.

Another Branch of the Arts

My grandchildren love the different voices of the wind chimes and bells hanging around my home. Sometimes, when the wind gusts, the chimes sound angry. In gentle breezes, they sound like the tiny voices of faeries. Whenever we hear them, they remind us that though we may not be paying attention, the wind is always up to something.

If you garden, you may have extra terra-cotta pots you can use for this project or pick some up at a garden center.

YOU'LL NEED:
A collection of clean, dry terra-cotta pots, large and small
Twine
Acrylic paint (water-soluble and quick-drying)
Paintbrushes (sizes 00 to 6, or larger if you're doing bigger designs)

Lay out your collection of terra-cotta pots—large pots will be the bells, and the small pots will be the clappers. Spend a rainy day together with your grandchild painting the pots (make sure they're clean and dry first) with acrylic paints. Allow them to dry overnight before touching them.

Cut a 3-foot length of twine and pass it through the pot's drainage hole and tie the twine in a fat double knot that will not slip back through the hole. Leave a tail of twine long enough to hang below the bottom of the pot. Slip a smaller terra-cotta pot onto the tail of twine, and tie another double knot inside the small pot to hold it in place, making sure that the little pot clapper will hit the side of the big "bell" pot.

Hang your bells from a tree branch, deck, or porch railing—where your child can ring them or where the wind will make its own music.

No child (or grown-up) can pass the chimes without ringing them.

Toad Cottage

The same terra-cotta pots that make great wind chimes are also perfect homes for one of the most helpful critters found in a garden, the lowly, but ever so lovable toad.

Some children are frightened of toads. I don't know if it's the big bulging eyes, the bumpy body, or the enlarged parotid glands, but toads send a shiver down many small spines. Of course, when you read Kenneth Grahame's *Wind in the Willows* to your grandchild, many of the unfounded fears will vanish. Who can resist Mr. Toad Esquire of Toad Hall?

I've learned that once a child does something kind for an animal, whether it is providing a birdbath, filling a feeder, or making a home for a spider, they feel invested in the critter, and they usually become more caring and less afraid. By helping your grandchild create a toad cottage, you'll make life easier for the toad and open little eyes to one of the most helpful creatures in a garden.

Mr. Toad Esquire abandoned Toad Hall for this snug little pot-cottage.

YOU'LL NEED:

A clean, dry terra-cotta pot (at least 6 inches wide)
Acrylic paint (water soluble)
Stiff brushes specifically for acrylic and oil (sizes 00 through 6)

Cover your worktable and turn the pot upside down. Use acrylic paint to decorate the cottage. (I like to add a "welcome" or a "do not disturb" sign.) Allow the cottage to dry thoroughly.

Ask your child to think like a toad and look for a cool, shady garden site for a cottage home. Once they've chosen a spot, set the cottage upside down in the shade and prop up one side with a rock or piece of wood so the toad can enter. You might not see Mr. Toad very often because he is very shy and retiring.

Rainsticks for a Rainy Afternoon

We stumbled on rainsticks, a primitive musical instrument, in a local craft gallery, and our grandkids couldn't put them down. The lightweight cactus-branch instruments of differing lengths were studded with thorns, which pierced through the walls of the cactus and into the hollow interiors. The sticks were filled with a variety of objects, from pebbles, rocks, and sand to an array of oddly shaped seeds. When the rainsticks were shaken, or turned upside down, the objects hit the cactus thorns, which diffused their sounds. As the children shook and turned the sticks, we could hear falling rain, hailstones, and rushing waters.

The history of rainsticks is as cloudy as a stormy day. Some believe that the natives of Chile and Ecuador used the instruments to call down the rains, that the Incas used these as tubular rattles, or that they originated in Africa. Whatever their origins, they are a huge hit with kids who can make them themselves—with a little help from Gran!

YOU'LL NEED:

Empty cardboard tubes from toilet-paper length to wrapping-paper length (Mailing tubes with end coverings are great.)

Colorful papers, stickers

Crayons, markers, or paint

Glue

Paper muffin cups

Rubber bands (thick)

The joy is in the process of making and decorating the rainsticks and the magical performances that will follow.

Packing tape
Aluminum foil
Small pebbles, beans, lentils, rice, seeds, coarse sand
Beads, feathers, ribbons, buttons, or shells

Cover a table work space with newspaper and have your art supplies within easy reach.

Decorate the outside of cardboard tubes with bits of paper, paint, crayons, stickers, or markers. Let the tube dry. Then place a muffin cup over one end, secure it with a rubber band, and wrap it with tape to hold it in place.

Tear off a piece of aluminum foil twice as long as the tube. Roll the aluminum foil into a thin snake and kink and twist it until it is like a long, loosely coiled spring. Push the spring of foil inside the tube (it should reach from end to end) to act as an inside sound diffuser.

Fill the tube with a few tablespoons of beans, lentils, pebbles, sand, or rice. Each ingredient has its own sound: The rice is light as a spring rain, the pebbles and beans sound like a summer downpour, and the lentils almost sound like rustling leaves in the rain. Cap the open end with another paper muffin cup, secure with a rubber band, then wrap it with tape. Once your rainstick is filled and capped, you can add more decorations, such as long strips of ribbon or twine, feathers, shells, beads, buttons, and bells. You can also paint or paste colorful papers on both ends.

You'll be amazed by how much joy and music these homemade rainsticks will provide.

Maracas and tambourines are simple enough for any child to play.

The Tin Can Band

Children have a natural urge to make music, whether it's clacking two sticks together, blowing in a bottle, or drumming on a pan or tin can. Music flows from them like a mountain spring. Encourage your grandchild to experiment with a variety of instruments, and dance and play alongside him. (Don't worry about dignity.)

You can find child-friendly musical instruments in toy stores, craft shops, import stores, and online catalogs. I first bought a xylophone, some flutes, and harmonicas from a fair trade store, then I added to the music basket with maracas, a tambourine, and drums made from empty tin cans ranging in size from soup cans, 28-ounce tomato sauce tins, and big restaurant-sized tins called #10, about 100 ounces. Last year I grew a big crop of gourds of all sizes and shapes. Once I dried them, my grandkids discovered that the seed-filled gourds make perfect rattles. The tin cans and gourds sound great together; each has a distinctive sound, from the sharp, loud hail on a tin roof to the muted gourd-seed rattles that conjure up images of rattlesnake tails and rustling corn.

This big basket of musical instruments is constantly in use both indoors and out.

Ephemeral Art

The first time I saw Andy Goldsworthy's ephemeral, nature-inspired art I shrieked with joy. Although his creations are thought-provoking, artistic, and sophisticated, they are also child-friendly and fun to copy. His works ignite a spontaneous spark of joy that infuses kids with their own natural creativity. Have you ever known a child who can pass up a pile of rocks or who isn't tempted to sculpt sand, scuff smooth soil, or play with leaves or twigs?

Visit your local library and sit down with your grandchild with a few big Goldsworthy photo-picture books. Check out your favorite one, and then take time to page through it and talk about the rock sculptures, leaf art, and twig art pictured. Choose an art project you like and look for a good place in your yard to construct it.

YOU'LL NEED:

A supply of rocks
Interesting twigs and branches
Flat stones
Seashells
Some flat sandy or smooth soil areas
Leaves
Flowers
Vines
Mosses
Lichen
Feathers

Dragonflies (maple seeds on a twig)

Collect various sizes of stumps and cut sections of branches to create natural pedestals for stacked rock sculptures and twig animals, bugs, and other whimsical works of art.

A spiral of freshly picked dandelion flowers

A rock "duck" from Peaks Island, Maine

A tree stump pedestal for rock sculptures

Pieces of stone stacked and leaned to create a sailboat

A "spider web" of branches and twigs

A bug made of rocks and twigs

Modern art twigs with torn autumn leaves

The Green Man, framed in twigs. Vines, leaves, and acorn eyes make up his face.

CLAY RECIPE

(for each child)
3 pieces of squishy white bread
¼ teaspoon water or lemon juice
¼ teaspoon liquid dish detergent
Bowl
Acrylic paints or gel food coloring
Rolling pin
Cookie cutters for shapes
Cookie sheet for drying sculptures

(for making bead jewelry)
Wire (for poking holes into beads)
Cord and thread
   (for stringing beads)
Glitter and sequins
Paintbrush

Ilyahna's painted clay
landscape

Sculpting with Clay

My grandchildren love working with clay. They sculpt people, beads, furniture, animals, and complete landscapes with trees, streams, and hills. One weekend evening, when they wanted to play with clay, our old supply was too hard for little hands to work. Since I didn't want to trek to the store, I turned to my trusty "recipe box" of crafts in search of an easy bread "clay" I made almost 20 years ago. Fortunately I had some squishy white bread on hand, which was all we needed to whip up a batch and begin creating. (See sidebar for ingredients.)

Your grandchild will love pulling off the crusts, tearing the bread into tiny pieces, and tossing them into a big bowl. Then add water or lemon juice and detergent and moosh and knead the ingredients together. If the clay is too dry, simply add a few more drops of water.

Use a rolling pin to flatten the clay and cookie cutters to make ornaments and shapes. The clay can be sculpted, hand rolled into beads for homemade jewelry, or formed into ornaments or tags for gifts.

Beads

Jewelry made from clay or handmade bread clay is so easy to make even a three-year-old can get involved in the process of rolling and forming shapes.

Lay a piece of kraft or wax paper onto a work surface, and create alongside your young artist. Roll beads of varying sizes, and make long, fat snakes, which will form tubular beads. Roll slender snakes and pinch the ends together to form a hoop.

Poke a piece of wire through the beads after rolling them and before they harden. Leave the beads strung onto the wire until they are thoroughly dry, and then decorate and paint them with water-soluble acrylics. Finally string them onto thread or cord. Store finished pieces on a wax paper–lined cookie sheet and allow them to dry.

Cover your beads and tubes with white glue and then quickly roll them across a small mound of glitter or sequins to give them a royal appearance. Allow them to dry thoroughly.

SPICE IT UP

During the holidays, we sculpt and create simple scented ornaments from our spice shelf. All you need are some ground spices (enough to fill one cup), canned applesauce, a cookie sheet lined with foil, and cookie cutters.

Mix 1 cup of ground spices (allspice, cinnamon, and cloves) into ½ cup of applesauce and stir. Add applesauce until the spice mixture is like bread dough. Sprinkle some ground spices onto a work surface, and let your child roll out the dough to a thickness of ¼ inch.

Cut out a variety of shapes, poke a hole in the top with a skewer, and transfer the ornaments to the cookie sheet. Decorate cutouts with seeds, small pods, raisins, and spices like cardamom, star anise, cloves, and cinnamon sticks.

Bake ornaments in a low oven (200° to 250°F) for an hour. Turn off the oven, but keep the cookie sheet inside overnight.

String the ornaments on a ribbon or cord and hang on a holiday tree or a package.

Worm Hotel

Okay, it's a rainy day, and you and your grandchildren have been indoors all afternoon doing craft projects, but everyone is going a little stir-crazy. So don your rubber boots, take a bucket, and go outside when there is a pause in the rain. You will notice that right after a rain, the sidewalks and gutters are filled with worms. Scientists think that the worms surface to escape drowning. Sadly, once they're in the sunlight they dry out and die.

You and your grandchild can become worm saviors. Fill your buckets with a bit of moist soil, grass, and leaves. Pick up stranded worms, gently drop them into the bucket, and transport them back to the garden or backyard. Bring a few worms indoors and put them into an old aquarium (this is your worm hotel) along with the moist soil, grass, and leaves.

Drape the hotel with dark fabric to keep the light out. In the morning, have your child sprinkle the soil in the aquarium with water. In the evening, lift the curtain and use your flashlight to see how the worms have built a network of tunnels visible along the sides of the aquarium. You may see what looks like a miniature worm city bustling below the soil. Tunnels and tiny mounds of castings (worm poop that looks like mini volcanoes) dot the worm landscape. Explain that this is what makes worms the best workforce in the garden; they aerate the soil with their tunnels and their castings make the soil and plants healthy.

You'll see how the worms carry food and you might be able to see egg cases and even some baby worms. After a week of watching, release your worms into a shady, moist area of your yard.

If your child is squeamish about handling the worms, just use a spoon or trowel to gently lift them.

Grab a flashlight and quickly unveil the worm hotel to spy on their quiet goings-on.

YOU'LL NEED:

Aquarium, terrarium, or big jar
Dark fabric piece (large enough to drape over entire aquarium)
Soil, grass clippings, shredded wet newspaper, crumbled leaves

Make Your Own Floral Paper

Y ears ago, I attended a papermaking workshop taught by a well-known artist. The class was exciting, the process a bit long, but the possibilities were limitless. For months, I worked to streamline the procedure enough so that I could pass on the basics of creating beautiful papers to children and their grown-up helpers.

I dived into the challenge and began to teach everyone from four-year-olds to octogenarians how to make gorgeous papers. The process was so simple that I was able to successfully make paper with a group of children on a national television program. Everyone, no matter what age, loved doing the work as much as the finished products—lovely, lumpy, herbal, floral, colorful, whimsical, sometimes fragrant, always different papers for doing art, making books, jotting notes, and writing letters.

You'll need to have your paper supplies, buckets, screens, and felts on hand and set up before doing this project. Having everything assembled will eliminate the "sit and wait quietly until I'm ready" that most kids can't stand. Papermaking can be done on a balcony or a deck, in a garage, a basement, a kitchen, or wherever you aren't afraid of a few drips or splashes.

Your grandchild will love the tactile pleasures of slopping through water loaded with paper and flowers, and will become surprisingly proficient at skimming and lifting out the one-of-a-kind works of art. If the paper doesn't suit you when it comes off the screen, just throw it back into the washtub, stir it up, skim your screen through the slurry, and lift out another sheet.

WIND WISHES

In my old Heart's Ease gardens, the children loved the elderberry tree spangled with paper wind wishes that danced in the slightest breeze. Sometimes, it was a heartbreaker to read the wishes they scribbled and hung. Use scraps of your beautiful handmade paper to write out a wish, a blessing, or a poem. Punch a hole in the top of the wish, and tie it loosely to a favorite tree or bush. If you want your child's wish to last longer, simply cover it with clear contact paper, which will protect it from the rain.

YOU'LL NEED:

Plastic bucket(s)
Large plastic cups
Blender
Pieces of pure rag paper (available at any craft supply or art store)
10-gallon tub (Rubbermaid works well), about 24 by 16 by
  8¾ inches
Premade screens with aluminum frames, or homemade wooden
  ones, small enough to fit and be moved, back and forth,
  inside the tub, about 12 by 15 inches
Large sponge
Four pieces of felt (slightly larger than the screened frame)
Two pieces of waterproof (sometimes called marine) plywood
  slightly larger than the felt

We don't measure when making paper. Like the traditional family soup pot, our buckets contain ingredients that change according to what is trimmed or harvested from the garden. Go exploring and carry a basket or bucket for gathering. Pick up wonderful leaves, fern fronds, herbs, flowers, mosses—whatever tickles your creative spirit. We love to use hollyhock, sunflower, cosmos, and rose petals. We once devoted ourselves to searching out perfect four-leaf clovers to press into our special papers.

Set aside any special specimens you want to preserve intact. Place your other plant material in a bucket, cover with water, and soak overnight so the fibers are broken down and mushy. Kids love the process of stirring the blend and sometimes whacking at fibers to speed the breakdown.

With the plastic cup, scoop the mushy pulp into the blender and fill halfway. Drop in a handful of small pieces of rag paper, which works as both a thickener and a binder. Cap the blender, turn it on low, and blend until the paper and flowers are mixed thoroughly. You may need to add more water to the mixture to help the blending process along. Your finished pulp should have the consistency of pancake batter—not too watery, not too thick.

Pour the blended pulp and water into your tub. Repeat the blending until you've processed enough pulp to fill the washtub two-thirds full. Now your child can sprinkle in some of the special reserved flower petals or little leaves to add texture to the blend. Stir thoroughly with little hands.

Submerge a screen horizontally into your tub, allowing the mixture to cover the screen. Slowly move the screen back and forth through the mixture as you lift it out of the water, keeping the screen horizontal. Try to cover the entire screen with a thin layer of pulp. Let it drain as you shake it gently from side to side, which will help strengthen the fibers in the paper. (The screen will be covered with a thin sheet of mushy pulp.) To embellish the surface of the paper, lay some vines, flowers, or leaves onto the surface and press them gently into the pulp with your sponge. Then press the paper with the sponge to remove the excess water, and keep wringing out the sponge and pressing it on the paper, to remove more water.

Place a piece of plywood on the ground. Dampen the sheets of felt, and stack two of them on the plywood. Gently turn your screen upside down over the felt and transfer your paper from the screen onto it. Cover with a couple of pieces of damp felt, and put another piece of plywood on top. It's sort of like a triple-decker sandwich. Press firmly on the stack with your hands to squeeze out excess moisture.

Let the paper set for 2 hours before removing it from the felt. Lay your paper on a flat surface to dry. Voilà! It's that simple and satisfying.

I grow these love-in-a-mist for papermaking and crafts projects. Start them from seed in spring, and they'll return yearly.

A Child's Own Book

When I was very young, my grandmother and I often made simple books from short stories I told her. She scribbled notes as I talked, asked questions about the stories, and then printed them on plain pages, which I embellished with my small drawings. I gave my tiny books to my family, and I thought they were the best gifts in the world, filled with my art and the story of life as I knew it. Now my own grandchildren are book creators, too. Sara just finished her first one, "The Little Red Hen." Vaguely familiar, but definitely her own version of the story.

This project is one of the easiest and gives your child a chance to record life and history as seen through young eyes. If you can't write fast enough to jot down your child's story, use your recorder and then transcribe it onto the book pages. Older children can write out their own words, but the younger ones will need your help. You may want to prompt the story by asking questions about a favorite family pet, a trip to a park, or an experience at school. Whatever you ask, just make sure you focus on the story and the storyteller. Everyone loves an audience and your interest fans the flames of their creativity.

YOU'LL NEED:

A collection of colorful papers, origami papers, watercolor papers
A bone folder (or a wooden craft stick) for crisp paper folds
Paper punch (for round holes)
Brass round-head fasteners or ribbon (thin enough to fit
    through holes)
Glue (for pasting pictures or drawings on pages. I use a pH neutral
    glue that is water soluble and acid free and will last for decades.)

What could be a better gift than a child's-eye view of life captured in a handmade book?

Supply your young artist with crayons, pencils, paints, or photos to finish decorating the book pages. Work together on a flat, clean surface, and carefully fold and crease the pages. Do the same with a heavier piece of paper for the cover.

Our books are made of unusual papers, folded in half, with holes punched in two places on the edge of the fold and tied with beautiful pieces of ribbon or held together with brass fasteners. The beauty of these books is in the simplicity, the process, and the long-lasting results.

Nature's Stained Glass Window

I saw one of these natural "stained glass windows" years ago, and it was hauntingly beautiful. The sunlight glimmered softly through the colorful flowers, leaves, and ferns, illuminating them so they glowed like sheets of fragile glass. I loved the window so much we had to make a few for our family. These are inexpensive and easy to create, and a window will last for years.

Take a walk together with your grandchild on a sunny, dry day, and bring your gathering basket. Search for the best and most colorful blooming flowers, dainty ferns, tassled grasses, and an array of leaves. Pick some of your favorites and gently stow them in your basket. When you return home, clean the flowers, ferns, and leaves with a soft, dry brush and press them between the pages in a heavy book.

YOU'LL NEED:

Flowers, leaves, ferns, grasses

Two sheets of acrylic glass or Plexiglas (available in frame shops, craft stores, home centers)

Aluminum duct tape (available in hardware stores)

HOLLYHOCK DOLL

Gather hollyhock flowers and buds of different colors. Pull out the pistil in the center of the bloom. Stack different colored blooms for skirt. Use a bud for the head, a flower for a hat, and twigs for arms. Attach with a toothpick.

pistil

Allow your specimens to dry thoroughly for a few days. Help your grandchild make an arrangement with his flowers and leaves on one sheet of the glass.

Carefully, so as not to dislodge anything, place the second sheet of glass on top. Doing one side at a time, lay half of your aluminum tape along the edge of the top sheet of acrylic, and carefully press it down and fold the tape around the edge of the other sheet, making sure to smooth it as you press. The tape will seal the two acrylic sheets together and make a beautiful, simple frame.

Prop your grandchild's creation against a window to highlight the shapes and colors of her natural stained glass work of art.

This window displays leaves from our walks together.

Leaf and Flower Collages

FOLLOW THE LEAF MAN

Browse through a copy of Lois Ehlert's book *Leaf Man* to see how she used leaves and other natural treasures to illustrate her book.

Oh, those unforgettable days of exploration and collecting for art projects. They are some of my favorite times with my grandchildren, who view each object they find as magical and exceptional. This is exactly how I want them to feel, rediscovering the mystery and miracle of nature every time they look closely at something.

Whenever you're out on one of your nature walks, be on the lookout for interesting shapes, colors, and arrangements of plants and leaves. If you look, you will see the faces in pansies, skirts and dresses in hollyhock flowers and Canterbury bells, hats or fingers in tubular plants, animal shapes, and hearts—the array is endless, and all these shapes lend themselves to the art of collage. Gently snip or pick some leaves and flowers that you like and place them in your basket. When you return home, clean your collection with a soft, dry brush, and blot the plants dry if they're moist.

On a piece of 8½-by-11-inch paper (try using colored construction paper), experiment with a variety of different flowers and leaves by arranging them into the shapes of animals, people, insects, landscapes, cars, and houses. Once you start moving and overlapping the shapes, you'll be surprised at the multitude of things you can create from your natural supplies.

When your design is in place, just lift each piece slightly and use a cotton swab to smear a drop or two of white glue underneath the plants to secure them. Use a dampened swab to clean up any extra glue.

To reproduce your collage for cards, bookmarks, or special wrapping papers, simply place the paper on a flatbed color copier or scanner and make decorative copies.

Lovely leaf lady with a bouquet

Dancing leaf man in a beret

The Memory Game

My grandchildren love to spend Saturday nights around the farm table in our kitchen. We haul out our board games or play lively rounds of the Memory Game with cards that we created together. Move over, Parker Brothers! The game helps familiarize them with the looks and names of neighborhood trees and flowers. I always lose, but that's okay. My grandchildren relish every minute of my humiliating defeats and they love to win. This is a game that kids love because with their young memories, they are inevitably better at it than adults are.

The best part of this memory game is that you and your child can make the cards yourselves. Homemade and free—what could be better? Just go outside, look, and gather leaves and flowers that interest you. Once you start looking, you may find that everything interests you.

YOU'LL NEED:

24 different specimens of flowers, leaves, grasses, and ferns
White glue
24 3-by-5 inch index cards
12 8½-by-11-inch sheets glossy photo-quality paper
   (10 mil or higher) or card stock
Color copy machine or computer scanner and printer
Scissors or paper cutter

Gather two dozen specimens or parts of plants (petals, fronds, seeds, etc.) small and flat enough to fix on a 3-by-5 index card.

Lightly glue a single specimen in the center of each card until all 24 cards are done. Let dry.

Lay four cards at a time, facedown, on the copier or scanner bed.

Make *two* copies or prints of each set of cards on a full sheet of photo paper or card stock.

Cut each reproduced specimen to the 3-by-5-inch size. You will have 2 copies of each card and a deck of 48 cards.

HOW TO PLAY THE MEMORY GAME

(for two to four players, ages 4 and above)

Shuffle cards. Lay cards facedown in four rows.

The first player turns over two random cards. If they match, the player keeps them and takes another turn. (Every time a player matches two cards, he is allowed another turn.) When no match is made, the next player takes a turn.

The game is over when all pairs are matched, and the player with the most matches wins.

maple seeds

dill

lady's mantle

sweet william

Mother Nature's Toy Chest

A rainy afternoon is the perfect time to haul out the basket of natural objects you've collected, and turn them into some simple toys and games invented and played by Native Americans.

Grasshopper Toy

Find a short, forked twig and a short piece of twig that will fit inside the fork. Stretch a fat rubber band around the Y.

Twist the twig around and around inside the band. Then set on the ground and watch it hop. Nudge it if necessary.

Huwawanani

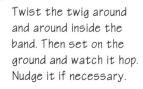

Drill or poke 2 holes in a circle of wood or cardboard. Thread string through the holes and the loops, as shown. Then, pull and pause, pull and pause and watch it twirl.

Early Lacrosse

You'll need two forked branches to make two racquets.

Make a net of cord or twine and tie it onto the racquet.

Make a "ball" by filling a piece of cloth or cut-off sock with grass. Tie ball closed.

To play: Draw a large circle on the ground. Both players stand inside the circle and bat the ball to each other. If one player misses the ball, the other player gets a point.

Loop Toss

You'll need a long twig or branch for each player (about the size of a ball bat).

Use cut-off socks or fabric stuffed with grass, rice, or beans.

Tie tops of balls to a piece of twine.

To play: You and a partner try to toss the double-ball-on-a-string back and forth without letting the balls touch the ground or your hands.

Walnut Dice

Collect walnut shells. Open and fill each half cavity with mud, glue, clay, or wax.

To play: Sit on the ground. One player throws an odd number of shells, and the players yell "round" or "flat." Whoever guesses the side of the largest number of shells facing up gets a point.

Flat = inside

Round = outside

Willow Rod and Ring

Soak willow rods overnight. Bend them into a ring and tie them securely.

To play: One person rolls the willow ring along the ground while the other tries to spear the ring through the hole.

String-a-Ma-Bob

Find a long branch to use as a spear

Tie on a piece of string or twine. Tie the other end of the string to a ring.

Swing the ring back and forth and around until you can catch it on your spear.

Letters from the Heart

July 2008 You are 6!

We were working together in the "Girl's Studio" & you got up & ran to the french door by the kitchen garden.

"Amma look!" you shouted. "That hummingbird is eating at those jasmine flowers."

We talked for awhile about what hummers eat & how they can fly up, down, backwards, & even upside down — you turned to me & said, "I think hummers are my most favorite bird."

We're going to try my flowered hat experiment on you! You'll have hummers perching & sipping on & around you —

We have 3 or 4 hummers in the kitchen garden right now!

Your surprise party at the park was wonderful! You looked so shocked when you saw the table all decorated.
May 2009.

Your keepsake letters will preserve memories that might otherwise be lost.

Don't you feel that whenever you're with your grandchild it's a special occasion? I love our quiet times and our adventures together and try to remember to record them in my journals or in a letter-from-the-heart, which I store in a special box.

I like it when my grandchildren let me know their take on our times together—whether we've gone to the zoo, a movie, museum, or on a nature hike. To preserve your grandchild's memories and feelings, you might talk about the play you've just seen, write some notes about his favorite art at the museum, and ask him to do a small sketch of it. Write a funny poem about a book or place, take photographs of each other when you're hiking, record some of your grandchild's thoughts, and transcribe them into one of your letters.

Whenever you find something of interest on a walk, you and your grandchild might jot down a few words in your journals, even if you're not quite sure what it is, tape a special flower onto the page, or do a quick sketch. (Please don't try to suggest anything to improve your child's work. *All* children's art is beautiful, free, and evocative.)

Date your letter, sign it, fold it, and tuck it into an envelope, but don't seal it. Store these letters in a child-crafted memory box (right).

Memory Box

I treasure my grandchildren's drawings, notes, and poems, which are tucked into colorful envelopes, and store them and my letters-from-the-heart in a memory box.

YOU'LL NEED:

Clean box (shoe boxes are the perfect size)
White glue
Acrylic paint
Bits of colorful paper, photos, stickers

Spend a rainy day with your grandchild decorating the memory box inside and out. You might glue on family photos, bits of tickets from events you've attended or places you've visited, or press wildflowers between clear contact paper and affix them to the box.

Even when we are separated by thousands of miles, I can slip an envelope out of the box and relive our adventures. These letters are a simple way to ensure that the history of our times together will be lifelong memories not only for them, but also for me.

Faretheewell

APPENDIX
Crown and Wizard's Cap Instructions

YOU'LL NEED:

Large sheets (at least 24 inches long) of
     construction paper, thin cardboard,
     or bristol board
Colorful papers or foil papers
Paints, markers, glitter, fake gemstones
Glue, tape, stapler

HOW TO MAKE THE CROWN:

Measure the circumference of your grandchild's head. Cut a 4-inch-wide strip of paper at least 2 inches longer than that measurement.

Cover the strip with foil or colored papers and glue them in place.

Decorate with paint, markers, cutout stars and moons, and glitter.

Cut a fanciful border for the top of the crown (see the suggested pattern below).

Close the paper circle of the crown with a strip of tape. Staple along the tape (to prevent it from tearing).

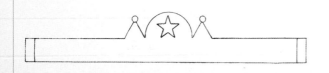

HOW TO MAKE THE WIZARD'S CAP:

Use a piece of construction paper 12 inches high and 24 inches wide.

Mark a midpoint at the top (12 inches from each side) and on each side (6 inches from top and bottom). Then, mark a point 6 inches from each side on the bottom. Connect the points with dotted lines, as shown.

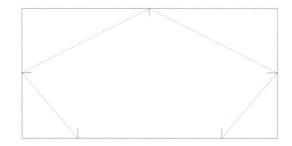

Cut along the dotted lines.

Overlap the points on the side ends and form a cone with the point at the top of the paper becoming the tip of the cap. As you roll the cone shape, be careful not to crease the paper. Adjust the amount of overlap to fit the child's head, and then staple to secure. Cover the staple and the overlapping seam with tape.

Decorate with foil paper, cutout stars, glitter, and gemstones.

INDEX